MY DAY
WITH
THE CUP

NHL Players Tell Their Stories
about Hometown Celebrations
with Hockey's Greatest Trophy

JIM LANG

Published by Simon & Schuster

NEW YORK   LONDON   TORONTO   SYDNEY   NEW DELHI

A Division of Simon & Schuster, LLC
166 King Street East, Suite 300
Toronto, Ontario M5A 1J3

Copyright © 2024 by Jim Lang

This Simon & Schuster Canada edition May 2024

SIMON & SCHUSTER CANADA and colophon are trademarks
of Simon & Schuster, LLC

Simon & Schuster: Celebrating 100 Years of Publishing in 2024

For information about special discounts for bulk purchases,
please contact Simon & Schuster Special Sales at 1-800-268-3216 or
CustomerService@simonandschuster.ca.

Interior design by Joy O'Meara

Manufactured in the United States of America

1   3   5   7   9   10   8   6   4   2

Library and Archives Canada Cataloguing in Publication
Title: My day with the Cup : NHL players tell their stories about hometown
celebrations with hockey's greatest trophy / Jim Lang.
Names: Lang, Jim, 1965– author.
Description: Simon & Schuster Canada edition.
Identifiers: Canadiana (print) 20230524176 | Canadiana (ebook)
20230562612 | ISBN 9781982194444
(softcover) | ISBN 9781982194451 (EPUB)
Subjects: LCSH: Stanley Cup (Hockey) | LCSH: Hockey players—Interviews.
| LCSH: National Hockey
League—Interviews. | LCGFT: Interviews.
Classification: LCC GV847.7 .L36 2024 | DDC 796.962/648—dc23

ISBN 978-1-9821-9444-4
ISBN 978-1-9821-9445-1 (ebook)

To my parents, and all the parents
who help their children achieve their goals

CONTENTS

Foreword

Winning the Stanley Cup must be a dream come true for any person who has put on skates. For a select few it becomes a reality.

After years of hard work, lots of teamwork, and a little luck, to be able to skate around the ice with the Stanley Cup hoisted over your head is, well, unimaginable for most. To stand on the ice and watch it happen and in a sense be a part of the celebration is where I come in!

As "Keeper of the Cup," the thrill and joy of walking the Stanley Cup onto the ice on the red carpet with fellow Hall of Fame caretaker Craig Campbell and being part of the celebration is something I will never take for granted.

However, winning the Stanley Cup is only the beginning. As everyone knows, when you are a part of a team (no matter what team it is) there are plenty of people involved behind the scenes who you don't see during those celebrations: parents, grandparents, siblings, best friends, teachers, bus drivers—the list goes on and on.

In hockey, it is the offseason for the Stanley Cup champion (although it seems short for them) that becomes one of the most satisfying moments of their career. As one of the greatest traditions in all of sports happens, each member of the winning team gets to take the Stanley Cup home and say thank you to those who have helped them along their path.

Craig, the rest of our crew, and I are there every step of the way. Everywhere the Stanley Cup goes, we go with it. To date, we have traveled to over thirty countries around the world. The highest mountains, the wonders of the world, cemeteries, arenas, lake houses, family homes, and of course the parties: we have been part of them all.

Each day is totally different and totally unique for the winner, a moment they will never forget, nor will I. Getting to know the family, friends, and their hometown and get a glimpse into the life of a Stanley Cup champion is truly amazing and something that I will cherish forever.

Hopefully some of the stories in this book will give you a little idea of how a champion spends their day. Enjoy!

Phil Pritchard
Keeper of the Cup
Hockey Hall of Fame

Introduction

Jim Lang *(center)* with Phil Pritchard *(left)* and Walt Neubrand

In the spring of 2021, my agent contacted me with a proposal. Simon & Schuster Canada wanted me to put together a book about players and coaches when they have their day with the Stanley Cup.

Assembling all the pieces took a long time. This was a journey that started in May 2021. Hockey being what is, the people I wanted to speak with were only available from May to September. After that, the grind of the NHL season prevented me from conducting any interviews. This is not a complaint, far from it. From May to September of 2021, 2022, and 2023, I had the privilege of speaking with some amazing individuals about what it was like when they had their day with the

Stanley Cup. By the time I was done, I had spoken to thirty players and coaches about their experience. During all my conversations, not once did anyone refer to the Cup as "it." It was always the Cup or the Stanley Cup. That speaks to the level of respect NHL players and coaches have for the Stanley Cup. More than anyone, they know how hard it is to become a champion. As one would imagine, everyone cherished their day with the Cup. While spending the day with the Cup meant the world to them, it meant more to the individuals to be able to share the Cup with family and friends and their hometown.

Other writers, like prolific hockey historian and author Kevin Shea and Sean McIndoe (*The Down Goes Brown*) from the *Athletic*, have written extensively about the storied history of the Stanley Cup. So, instead of going on about that long and storied history, I wanted to write about something different. I wanted to hear players and coaches describe what it was like when they had their day with the Cup. We think we know players and coaches in the NHL. But when you hear them talk in detail about how much family and friends mean to them and how much sharing the Cup means to them, you realize that what you see on TV is very different from the person you will read about in this book.

Most fans don't realize this, but there are three Stanley Cups. The original is kept in a vault at the Hockey Hall of Fame. The second Cup is what the Hall refers to as the "Presentation Cup." This is what fans see when NHL commissioner Gary Bettman presents the Stanley Cup to the winning team after they win. This is the trophy that players, coaches, and other team personnel get to spend a day with after they win the Cup.

The third trophy is on display at the Hall of Fame when the second trophy is traveling. According to the Hall of Fame, as of early 2023, the Stanley Cup had visited thirty-one countries. The NHL started engraving names on the Stanley Cup in 1924. Currently, the names of thirteen teams can fit on one band on the Cup. That works out to sixty-five years' worth of team names on the Stanley Cup. Once a band is filled, it is removed and placed in the Hockey Hall of Fame and a new band is added. The next time a band will be removed from the Cup is in 2030. And yes, that band includes the 1966–67 Toronto Maple Leafs.

Every single person I interviewed spoke about the power and the magic of the Stanley Cup. After you see the Cup in person and you witness the effect it has on people, you understand what they mean. The Stanley Cup is unlike any other trophy in professional sports. And the prize of spending a day with the Cup is a powerful motivator for anyone who ever becomes a part of an NHL team. Everyone I spoke to was adamant that the quest to win the Stanley Cup and the chance to spend a day with the Cup were more important to them than any money that they make playing in the NHL A lot of very wealthy hockey players never had the privilege of spending a day with the Cup. Initially, Sidney Crosby had agreed to spend about fifteen minutes on the phone with me, talking about his days with the Stanley Cup. But those three times that he got to spend with the Stanley Cup mean so much to Crosby, we spoke for over thirty minutes.

Those lucky players and coaches who have won the Stanley Cup and have their names engraved on the Cup are part of an exclusive fraternity. Players who have never won are forbidden from touching or drinking out of the Stanley Cup. This is not written down anywhere, but it is an ancient rule of the NHL that players deeply respect.

I feel incredibly lucky that I was able to play a part in helping to tell their story. I hope that you enjoy the book as much as I did when I put it together. The Stanley Cup should never be compared to any other trophy. Especially when you witness the emotion of a ninety-nine-year-old woman when she runs her tiny finger along the Stanley Cup and realizes that her last name, the same last name as her grandson, will live on in hockey history.

CHAPTER 1

The Keeper of the Cup

Mike Bolt brings the Cup to the White House

Most people have heard of the popular TV show *Dirty Jobs*, starring Mike Rowe. In it, Rowe looks at people and their tough work—everything from a sewer inspector to an alligator egg collector has been featured on the show.

On the other end of the spectrum, there's another kind of job. It's no less exhausting and demanding, but for the select few who are called, being a Keeper of the Cup is one of the best jobs there is.

It didn't take long for the organizers of the summer Cup tour to realize that the job was far too demanding for one person. Mike Bolt from the Hockey Hall of Fame is one of those few. Bolt's job is to travel around the world and hand-deliver the Stanley Cup to a member of the winning team for what they often refer to as one of the greatest days of their life.

A lifelong hockey fan, Mike Bolt was born in Toronto and grew up in the neighborhood of Leaside. Beyond that, Bolt's path to the Cup is unique, to say the least. Bolt played some hockey in Leaside and in Pickering, east of Toronto, but never at a high level. He graduated from the hotel management course at George Brown College, yet never worked a day in his life in a hotel.

"I used to sell cowboy boots and western apparel. The whole fad had died out and we started losing money, so I had to shut down the store. From there, I started working at a retail toy company that had a bunch of stores in Toronto," said Bolt.

While all this was going on, in 1995, Bolt started working part-time at the Hockey Hall of Fame, in the events department. A friend of Mike's heard about the job opening at the Hall and encouraged Mike to go for it. In the beginning, he worked a lot of evenings and weekends.

"Eventually, I started to do a variety of different jobs at the Hall. Then I moved to special projects, where I started to do some traveling. In 2000, I started traveling with the Stanley Cup," says Bolt.

During a typical year, Mike will travel well over 150,000 kilometers with the Cup.

Bolt's first big trip with the Cup took him to northern Michigan, home of Randy McKay from the New Jersey Devils. Prior to that, Mike had been with the Devils when they won the Cup, assisting the head Keeper of the Cup, Phil Pritchard. That included helping Phil with the celebrations and the parade.

"I had been with the team already and I got to know the guys.

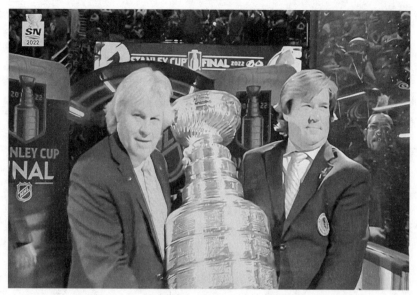

Phil Pritchard and Mike Bolt

Randy's day with the Cup was really cool for a number of reasons. He had a house that was being built and he had two parties," said Bolt.

"He had a party with his friends and family the first night. The second night he had the Cup, he had a party for all the people that worked on building his house. He had the electricians, the plumbers, the roofers, every single person that worked on that house was invited to that party. During the party, the workers explained that they were scrambling to get the house ready on time. Every time the Devils won another round, it gave them some breathing room to complete the job! All the workers said they needed Randy to go to the Stanley Cup Final to get the house done."

Bolt realized the power of the Stanley Cup on that first trip with McKay.

"When I started, there was no curfew with the Cup, and we would go around the clock with the players. During Randy's time with the Cup, it was three o'clock in the morning and Randy and about seven of his buddies were sitting around the kitchen table, having a few beers. I told them I was going to lie down for a few minutes. As I was lying there, I could hear them telling hockey stories. Every twenty minutes or so, Randy would look at them and say, 'Guys, the fucking Cup is sitting in my kitchen! Are you freaking kidding me?' To see how excited Randy was to have the Stanley Cup in his home was incredible. It was his second time winning the Cup, and the power of the trophy was not lost on him. It was an unbelievable thing to witness."

Two decades into the job, Bolt has seen the same reaction from every player when he brings the Cup to them for their day in the summer after they win.

"Nineteen years after my first trip with Randy McKay, when I was touring the Cup for the St. Louis Blues, it was the exact same reaction for Ryan O'Reilly, Alex Pietrangelo, and all those guys. They were all so excited to have the Stanley Cup in their presence and get to spend a day with it. It is hard to put into words what we see and what we get to be a part of when we arrive with the Cup at a player's house.

"I find it very humbling that I am a small part of their day. I feel lucky to be a part of every visit. I am lucky to be a part of the NHL and the Hockey Hall of Fame. When I show up, I get to be part of one of the greatest days of their life. Most players will tell me it is the greatest day of their life. One player's wife joked, 'What about when we got married?' The player said, 'Well, honey, I have been dreaming of this day since I was seven years old. I wasn't dreaming of getting married when I was seven!'"

Bolt is always amazed at the planning that goes on before he arrives with the Stanley Cup.

"The players and their families plan their day with the Cup like they would plan a wedding. Usually when you have a wedding, you might send out a hundred invitations. Often around eighty will come back and say yes. When you send out invitations to spend time with the Stanley Cup, one hundred percent of the invitations come back yes. Often, they will ask if they can bring two other guests. It is an amazing thing to hear guys talk about how their wedding was not as big a deal as their day with the Stanley Cup."

Hockey is very much an international sport now and that means the Keeper of the Cup spends most of his summer racking up the air miles traveling around the world.

"In 2000, my very first year traveling with the Cup, I went over to the Czech Republic for Patrik Elias and Petr Sykora. We didn't even have to go through customs. We were met as we got off the plane with the Cup and taken down the back stairs and entered this massive press room. We wheeled the Cup around and unlocked it from the travel case and took it out. That kicked off a press conference about the Stanley Cup and we were doing interviews. They handed us our passports and hustled us into two cars. We never did clear customs. We went all over the Czech Republic doing events, and tens of thousands of people were coming out to these staged events with the Cup. I was blown away by the reaction. I know how big hockey is in Canada and in the United States. But when I got to Europe, it went to a whole different level.

"One of the first overseas countries I took the Cup to was Ukraine, for Ruslan Fedotenko. I ended up meeting the president of Ukraine. I was with the Cup the first time it went to Slovakia; that was amazing. When you arrive with the Cup in Ukraine or Slovakia or the Czech Republic, it is national news, and it is in every newspaper, and it is on the nightly newscasts. I took the Cup to Slovenia for the first time when Anze Kopitar had his day with the Cup. Thousands of people would show up, just to see Kopitar with the Cup.

"But the longest trip I have taken with the Cup took place in the summer of 2019 with Vladimir Tarasenko of the St. Louis Blues. I took the Cup to a city called Novosibirsk, which is a four-hour flight east of Moscow. The city is deep into eastern Russia, not too far from the Mongolian border."

Like most people traveling there for the first time, Bolt realized that flying in Russia is different than what most people are used to when flying in North America.

"We were taking a flight in Russia one time and Phil [Pritchard], the other Keeper of the Cup, and I had checked the Cup in the luggage. The flight attendants came up to us in our seats and said, 'The pilots want to see the Cup!' We looked at her and explained that we checked it. Then she said that we must come with her. We got the Cup out of baggage and took it out of the road case and brought it to the cockpit. We were taking pictures with the pilots and the Cup. Afterwards we repacked it and they put it away for the flight.

"We got back to our seats, and I looked at Phil and said, 'Did you smell that?'

"He said, 'Yup.'

"The pilots had been drinking! Welcome to Russia.

"We didn't get upset. We just shrugged our shoulders and realized that life in Russia, and life in other countries, is different."

There are always surprises on the road, but the key to traveling around the world with the Stanley Cup is planning, planning, and more planning.

"We plan the Cup tour like they plan a tour for a rock band. Obviously, we don't have as many people to move around. But the timing is the same. We will finish up with a player at midnight, head to a hotel. We often book hotels closer to the airport. We grab a few hours of sleep, then take the first flight out in the morning and head to the next stop. With our visit with Tarasenko, we got into our hotel at three in the morning. We got up two hours later and got on a plane in Moscow for the long flight to Novosibirsk. As soon as we landed, we hit the ground running.

"Every Cup visit is nonstop. If you miss a flight, or a flight gets canceled, it will cut into a player's day with the Cup. There is the odd guy who has missed his day. The Cup didn't make it to their place, and we had to go on to the next stop. It is a horrible thing when it happens, but it can happen."

To put these summers in perspective, consider that when the Rolling Stones toured North America in 2019 for their No Filter tour, they played seventeen shows between July 8 and August 30. An impressive undertaking, especially for a legendary band starring a group of musicians in their seventies. But it pales in comparison to what the Stanley Cup goes through every summer. And instead of a massive road crew that handles any logistical and technical problem that comes their way, it's just the Keepers, like Mike. While sometimes they travel solo, often two people are entrusted to make sure hockey's holy grail gets to its appointed destination on time.

"Phil Pritchard [of the Hockey Hall of Fame] does most of the organization of the summer Cup tour. He coordinates with the winning team where the Cup is going to go. Then I execute the actual days with the Cup. Phil starts working with the winning team, right after they win. And they start planning the tour geographically. We don't want to be in Toronto one day, then in Vancouver the next day, and then on to California. We try to stick to geographical regions the best that we can. We can't always plan it that way because certain things get in the way. There are seven or eight Saturdays available on the Cup tour, and everyone wants the Cup on a Saturday. Usually, the coveted Saturday Cup visits go by seniority. For example, if you are the senior guy in Ontario, you get to decide when the Cup comes to Ontario. If you're the senior guy in Sweden, you decide when it is coming to Sweden."

The St. Louis Blues' Cup tour in the summer of 2019 presented the Keepers with a few challenges.

"We had the Cup in Aurora, Ontario, with Robert Thomas after the

Blues won. We wrapped our visit in Windsor, Ontario, with one of the assistant coaches, then we arrived in London, Ontario, at three in the morning. We checked into the hotel and when we woke up in the morning, they had no water. They were doing work in the area, and we only had two hours of sleep and we needed a shower. We were looking down the barrel of another eighteen-hour day, and with no shower.

"I called up Robert and said, 'Robbie, I got good news and bad news for you. The good news is that you are getting the Cup an hour early.'

"He said, 'What's the bad news?'

"I tell him, 'You have to provide showers for us, because we are stinky!'

"Rob was all for it. He was just happy to get the Cup an hour earlier than planned. They took good care of us, and we had a good visit with him in Aurora.

"At the end of his day, we stayed at the Sheraton hotel near Buttonville airport in Markham. Well, doesn't the fire alarm go off and kept going all night long! These are the trials and tribulations that we go through as we tour the Cup around the world for the winning team. We can't let it bother us because we have to be on every day. No matter how we feel or how little sleep we got, when we arrive at the next player's house, they are about to have the biggest day of their lives."

As a Keeper you will suffer from a lack of sleep, but you end up eating well.

"I have to say, we get fed well throughout the summer, there is no doubt about it. However, there are days when there is a young player, and they go hard with drinking beer out of the Cup. I will gently remind them that it is a workday for me, and I need to eat something."

And Keepers like Mike sometimes need to remind players of something else too.

"Every once in a while, we tell the player you cannot do a certain thing with the Cup. We just ask them to be smart and responsible and respectful. I have seen the Cup in few swimming pools over the years. We don't mind when they bring the Cup to the pool deck. We get upset when we see the Cup in the water. It is not good for the Cup. You are talking about a trophy that is well over a hundred years old. You can't treat it that way."

There's another consistent part of the job.

"After every visit we have to give the Cup a good cleaning. During the season, we give it a good polish. Too much silver polish isn't good for the Cup. We find the best thing is some soap and water and give a good clean and polish. It's necessary, especially during the summer when a lot of beer and champagne is being drunk from the Cup. (By

Will Ferrell and Mike Bolt

the way, for those wondering, it takes fourteen cans of beer to fill the Cup.) After beer and champagne, food is the next most popular thing consumed out of the Cup. Over the years, I have seen Jell-O, spaghetti and meatballs, poutine, lobster bisque, sushi, ice cream sundaes, and a lot of different cereals eaten out of the Cup."

But while some patterns repeat, there is no such thing as a typical day with the Cup.

"I am with the player and the Cup the whole time. Whether there are two of us or just one of us, there is always a Cup guy there with the player and the trophy. It doesn't matter if it is a player, coach, trainer, or part of upper management, or the team owner: we are always there with the Cup.

"I have been on different aircraft and helicopters. I was in a huge Chinook helicopter flying over Afghanistan with General Rick Hillier, the Stanley Cup, and former Montreal Canadiens forward Réjean Houle. We were heading over to some of the troops stationed at another base. Whether it is a camp, or soldiers far from home, or a hospital, the Cup cheers people up and they forget for a moment all of their troubles and worries. The Cup has certain powers that are hard to explain. I've seen firsthand the joy the Cup can bring to people who are in a cancer ward. There are some private moments the players have with the Cup that I take a step back and let them be. Whenever a player takes the Cup to a grave site, or they go into a house with a sick relative, I don't need to be there. In those kinds of somber, private moments, I don't worry about the safety of the Cup."

One of the perks of being the Keeper of the Cup is seeing some things and meeting some people you usually don't find at an NHL arena.

"When Adam Burish won the Cup with the Blackhawks in 2010, we brought the Cup to his hometown in Wisconsin. All of a sudden, out of the woods, came the University of Wisconsin marching band! As a Canadian you see these American college football games and I have always loved the big marching bands and the halftime show. To see that big band come marching out of the woods was so cool. Once they finished playing, they all took pictures with the Cup.

"Thanks to the Stanley Cup, I have met everyone from actor Eric Stonestreet from *Modern Family* to actor David Boreanaz to Academy Award winner Russell Crowe. When I met him for the first time, Crowe was very excited to see the Cup. Tom Hanks walked out on the beach in Malibu to see us when he heard the Cup was there with Chris Chelios. Hanks was so excited to see the Cup and then he looked at us and said, 'Oh, the white-gloves guys, you guys are awesome!' Tom Hanks knows who the white-glove guys are! I was shocked. I met Michelle Pfeiffer and her husband, David E. Kelley. Kelley is a writer and a former hockey player. His brother is one of the top scouts for the Blackhawks. Michelle was also a big hockey fan."

Bolt has also traveled with the Cup to the most famous address in America, 1600 Pennsylvania Avenue: the White House.

Sylvester Stallone with Bill Wellman of the Hockey
Hall of Fame and Mike Bolt

"I have met a few presidents along the way. I have been with the Cup for White House visits with George W. Bush and with President Obama. Obama was awesome; he had so much charisma and character. He was witty and funny, and it made for a great visit. Even Bush had a lot of character and was nice."

However, a certain vice president did not appreciate the presence of Bolt and the Stanley Cup.

"One time we were at the White House when Bush was president and I got there with the Cup, three hours early. This was in 2003 and I was waiting in the Rose Garden for the New Jersey Devils to arrive. I was there the year before with the Detroit Red Wings, so the White House staff knew me a little bit. I was a little bored, sitting around and waiting for everything to get under way. Bush's dog, Barney, came out on the White House lawn, and I started playing with him. I was throwing a tennis ball around and Barney would go get it and bring it back to me. All of a sudden, the Secret Service started yelling at me, 'Mike, Mike, get over here!' I was so scared, what have I done?

"I walked over and said, 'Oh my God, I am so sorry.'

"The Secret Service looked at me. 'No, just do me a favor, go play with the dog somewhere else.'

"I said, 'Absolutely, no problem!'

"I went to another area to play with the dog and the Secret Service agent came over and said, 'By the way, the reason I had to kick you out of there is [Dick] Cheney got mad at you for distracting Bush when they were talking in the Oval Office!' Bush kept looking out at me playing with his dog and he wasn't listening to Cheney!"

For a Texan, Bush loved hanging out with hockey players.

"Bush was a cool guy. After he finished his meet-and-greet with the Devils and was done with the reporters, he surprised everyone. The Devils were thanking him, and he said, 'Hey, do you guys want to see the Oval Office?' Everyone said yes, of course. Bush goes, 'Bring your wives, let's go!' The Secret Service wasn't expecting that to happen, and they got a little stressed. But it was all good and we all piled into the Oval Office.

"Bush was like a kid in the candy store, explaining everything to everyone there. He showed us items that different world leaders had given them. He said he had a phone in his office that he could talk to any US Navy ship in the world!

"I have been to the White House thirteen times with the Stanley Cup, and I think it is awesome every time that I go. It never gets old."

Year after year, Bolt takes the Stanley Cup on its summer tour. The reaction is almost universal.

"When I open up the case and I take out the Stanley Cup, I often see the father of the player, or his grandfather, get very emotional. I have gone into events with the Stanley Cup, and I could see people in the crowd tearing up. The Stanley Cup is a rock star, and it has a certain aura about it. There is nothing else like it in the world that has that kind of attraction and magnetism and emotion attached to it."

CHAPTER 2

The Stanley Cup Goes on the Road

1995 New Jersey Devils
Ken Daneyko, Bill Guerin, and Randy McKay

Mr. Devil

Ken Daneyko was drafted by the Devils in the first round (eighteenth overall) in the 1982 NHL entry draft. He arrived in New Jersey as a nineteen-year-old in 1983 and he never left. He embraced his new adopted city and home and was determined to live up to the expectations that come with being drafted so high. But there was a long road ahead.

Long before the Devils were a perennial playoff team, they were the bottom feeders of the NHL. In November 1983, Wayne Gretzky had an eight-point night as the Oilers beat the Devils 13–4. Even for Gretzky in those days, that was a lot of points. Afterwards, he called out the Devils, saying, "They had better stop running a Mickey Mouse organization and put somebody on the ice." But even by the 1986–87 season, the Devils were tied for the fewest points in the NHL.

Things did begin to improve. In the 1987–88 season, the Devils started making the playoffs and Devils fans took to wearing Mickey Mouse ears every time that Gretzky played in New Jersey. Making the playoffs was only a first step. The Devils nearly went to the Cup Final in 1994, but famously fell to the New York Rangers in the Conference Finals (the Rangers went on to win the Cup that year). Things finally changed the next year during the lockout-shortened 1994–95 season. Coach Jacques Lemaire demanded that his players sacrifice offense for defense. He famously introduced the neutral zone trap to the NHL, and once the Devils had a lead, it was all but over for the opposing team.

Under the firm hand of Lemaire, the Devils not only made the playoffs but lost only four postseason games in their unrelenting march toward Stanley Cup glory. By this time, Daneyko was well established as one of the toughest defensive defenseman in the NHL. Opposing forwards would pay a dear price if they ran into goalie Martin Brodeur. Better yet, the Devils swept the heavily favored Detroit Red Wings in four games in the Cup Final. For the first time in the history of the franchise, the New Jersey Devils were Stanley Cup champions.

Afterwards, Daneyko couldn't wait to get his turn with the Cup.

That summer was the first year the NHL did an official supervised Cup visit with each winning player and coach. After hearing some of the stories about what happened the previous summer in New York, Daneyko understood why they needed a chaperone.

"The Keeper of the Cup came to be after the Rangers had the Stanley Cup. There were reports the Rangers had a little too much fun with the Cup in 1994. After that, they decided it would be a good idea to have someone watch over the Cup.

"In 1995, we took the Cup on the David Letterman show, we took it to Yankee Stadium, and we did so many good things as a team. Individually, we were able to share it with family and friends and the fans.

"The first time I had the Cup in 1995, I ate Honey Nut Cheerios with my daughter out of it. She was young at the time, but she knew we'd done something special, and I wanted her to share in all the excitement. Of course, I invited friends to enjoy the celebration too, but for me, it was more about sharing the Cup with the fans than with just my family and friends." Daneyko had the Cup in his hometown in New Jersey and took it around the state.

"Even if you were a casual fan, the Stanley Cup has a certain magnetism to it. Everybody that saw the Cup that summer, the buzz around it was unbelievable. We would start with a group of ten people with the Cup, and before you knew it, there would be over a hundred people around you that wanted to get a picture with the Cup.

"I am from Canada, but I started my NHL career in New Jersey at the age of nineteen and I grew up here. My life was in New Jersey from a young age. Thankfully, I was blessed enough to be part of three teams that won the Cup, because I had to make sure that every fan in the entire state of New Jersey had the opportunity to drink out of the Cup or take a picture with it. I took a lot of pride in living in New Jersey, and I love the state."

Daneyko remembers what a long road it was.

"Playing in the NHL, winning the Stanley Cup is the ultimate goal as a player. I remember as a ten-year-old kid, carrying around a silver garbage can over my head after we won a road hockey game, pretending it was the Stanley Cup. I was with the Devils for twelve years before we won the Cup, and there were some lean years. Along with me, there was John MacLean and Bruce Driver. All three of us kind of grew up together as kids when we joined the Devils, and we all went through those tough times. After being a part of a team that struggled like that, it was a little more gratifying winning the Cup knowing what we went through to get there. A lot of times you play through those tough years, and you have to reshape your team and your friends go and good players go.

"I was part of the foundation of that team, and I had a good rapport with the fans in New Jersey. I was a blue-collar type of guy and the people in the state could relate to that. We knew that winning the Stanley Cup went a long way to putting hockey on the map in New Jersey. I wanted to enjoy it with the fans, and I tried to take the Cup everywhere.

"I took it to the Jersey Shore and thousands of fans ended up coming there and it was fantastic. For those who don't know, the Jersey Shore is the official summer playground of New Jersey. New York has the uppity Hamptons; New Jersey has the down-to-the-earth Jersey Shore. I must have stood there for at least six hours, taking pictures with the fans and the Cup. I wasn't going to let one fan who had been standing in line miss out on getting a picture with the Cup.

"We took the Cup to businesses and car dealerships and restaurants. I also had a party at my house with close family and friends. I did a lot in those twenty-four hours that I had the Cup, and I took every second of it without any sleep, just to make sure that everybody got an opportunity to celebrate with us. I know most players take the Cup back to their hometown. I know the Cup goes all over the world. For me, it was all about sharing the Cup with New Jersey. I left home at a young age to play junior hockey and I built my life in New Jersey. After I joined the Devils, I didn't go back to Canada. I would visit my parents now and then, but New Jersey was home. So, when I finally won the Cup, my family had to come to New Jersey to celebrate with me."

For a kid who grew up in Alberta, Daneyko was thinking of an Original Six team when he took time to look at names on the Cup.

"I was a Maple Leafs fan growing up, and I was only three years old when they last won the Stanley Cup. When I had some quiet time with the Cup, I looked for names like George Armstrong. I looked for the Montreal Canadiens' names as well. Players like Larry Robinson, Guy Lafleur, and our coach in 1995, Jacques Lemaire. And then I won another Cup in 2000 with Robinson as our coach. Robinson and Lemaire had won the Cup so often as players, their tutelage was instrumental to our team.

"I also looked at the Edmonton Oilers names from the mid-eighties. Mark Messier was a big mentor of mine when I was a young player. We both grew up in the Edmonton area and I first met Mark when I was around twelve years old, and he was a player I looked up to. Even though we became big rivals when he joined the Rangers, in those early years when I was trying to establish myself as an NHL player, he helped me.

"Those Oilers teams during that era were incredible. When Mark won the Cup in Edmonton, I celebrated a bit with him when I went back home. He would see me and say, 'You want to drink out of the Cup? Do you want a picture with the Cup?' I would immediately say, 'No, no, I am going to win that on my own one day.' I was around the Cup as a young player because of those Oilers teams, but I *never* touched it, I never drank out of it, and I never took a picture with it. I told myself I couldn't do any of that until we won it someday with my team, the Devils."

The Devils would go on to win the Cup three times, with three different coaches. Not only was each team led by a different coach, but the path to each victory was also unique.

"All three times with the Stanley Cup were a little different. Although, it was a big party every time! After you win the Cup, you are at the end of such an exhausting and long year. The first one was fantastic, because it was the first time. The whole experience was a big whirlwind and a big party. That 1995 team was a real character team. The second time was different in a few ways. In 2000 when we won, that was probably our deepest and most talented team we had in New Jersey. Also, I understood more what it took to win a Cup. That time, in summer 2000, I let it soak in a little more. When I had a day with the Cup that summer, I spent a little more quiet time and quality time with it. Don't get me wrong, I still took it everywhere throughout New Jersey. But I tried to appreciate more what an accomplishment our team had done.

"Winning the Stanley Cup a second time, five years after the first, is special. Both from my playing days, and now as an analyst, I know how difficult it is to win in the playoffs. It is not always the best team that wins it all. It is not always a team that you expect to win. That is the beauty of the Stanley Cup playoffs. In 1995, we were a big underdog. We didn't have the best skill or talent, but that year, we were the best *team*. In 2000, I knew how good we were, and the Cup was ours to lose. Fortunately, we were still able to fight through everything and all the adversity that you go through in the playoffs to make sure that happened."

And then, just three years later, the Devils won again.

"The third time I won the Cup, in 2003, was extremely special. My last game in the NHL was a game seven and we went out on top. That was a dream come true. When they handed me the Cup that night, I hung on to it a little longer than normal. I skated around the rink, and I went to every fan by the glass and let them share the moment. I knew it was over for me and my career was winding down. I couldn't have gone out in a better way.

"And for the third time, I kept the Cup in New Jersey when it was my turn. That year, I soaked in my day with the Cup the most, because

I knew my playing career was over. It was incredible to win, and I was exhausted. I knew that was it for me. I played for the Devils for twenty years. I can't remember all the fans. But whatever the number of Devils fans there are in the state of New Jersey, I probably got to half of them over the three times that I had my day with the Stanley Cup! That is what I wanted to do. I always thought it wasn't just about the nineteen thousand fans in the arena; it is all fans throughout the state who don't go to the games, and they watch us on TV. I took the Cup from the top of northern New Jersey all the way down to the furthest part of the southern tip.

"It is amazing to think we won three Cups in New Jersey with three different coaches. You don't see that very often, especially in that short of a time frame. That in itself was special. When we won the third time, there were five of us that were a part of all three Stanley Cups. Me, Martin Brodeur, Sergei Brylin, Scott Niedermayer, and Scott Stevens. The five of us have a special bond whenever we see each other.

"To win the Cup three times, in the modern NHL, is a big deal. It is tough to keep teams together for that long, so we had a pretty good core for that eight-year run. The parties and all the fun after you win the Cup is nice but sharing it with the fans is really what it is all about.

"By the third Stanley Cup, after my day with the Cup was done, I was exhausted. After all the fun and all the photos and all the fans drinking out of the Cup, I thought to myself, *Geez, I'm glad I'm retired. I don't know if I could win it one more time!* I know some people might think I'm crazy, but at the end of your twenty-four hours with the Cup, you are exhausted. My family and friends would roll their eyes when I would tell them that. I knew it was a good problem to have, but all those parties and all those celebrations with the Cup, it was quite a grind. The twenty-four hours with the Cup can feel like a week."

As someone who got to spend time with the Cup three separate times, Daneyko has a number of photos that make him smile. However, there is one that stands out among the rest.

"I have photos of my kids when they were young, sitting in the Cup. My daughter was a year old when we won the Cup in 1995. In 2000, my son was also a year old when we won. My daughter is in her twenties now and we have a special feeling when we look at those photos together.

"Some of my favorite photos with the Cup are the ones in the dressing room right after you win. Those photos with your teammates mean everything. That is what it is all about, being a team. When we won the Cup in Dallas, the wrestler Goldberg ended up in a photo with us in the dressing room."

Winning the Cup also brought about some bittersweet memories for Daneyko.

"My mom passed away after we won all three of our Cups. She was able to celebrate them with us, especially the first time that I won. I preached to my mom since I was seven years old, at least fifty times a day, I would tell her that I am going to play in the National Hockey League, and I am going to win a Stanley Cup. My mom would always go, 'Yeah, yeah, Kenny.' My mom was a quiet and petite lady, and I don't know if she ever thought my dream was real. She was probably tired of hearing me say the same thing every day from when I was seven years old until I had to move away from home at fifteen to play junior. When I saw her posing with the Cup for the first time, I looked at her and said, 'I told you!' Every time I see that picture of my mom with the Cup, it makes me happy."

That's easy to understand. She got to celebrate the realization of her son's lifelong dream, all three times. And because of Daneyko's generosity and love of his adopted home, so did the entire state of New Jersey.

The Cup Comes to the Upper Peninsula

A short drive to the shores of Lake Superior, the town of Houghton is an hour away from the most northern point of Michigan. To drive from Houghton to Detroit would take you over eight hours, assuming you don't hit any traffic.

It's also the home of Michigan Tech University, where forward Randy McKay played college hockey. Life there was very different from his hometown of Montreal. The beauty of this remote area, known in the state as the Upper Peninsula, must have made a big impression on him because after he graduated, he decided to make Houghton home. He never left. When the New Jersey Devils swept the Detroit Red Wings in the 1995 Stanley Cup Final, McKay couldn't wait to bring the Cup to share with the people of Houghton.

The year before, the Devils suffered that painful game seven loss in the Conference Final against Mark Messier and the Rangers. Going into the 1995 playoffs, the only people who believed the Devils could go all the way were sitting in New Jersey's dressing room.

"Even though we didn't have a great regular season, we still believed we had a chance to get just as far as we did the previous year," says McKay.

A fifth seed going into the playoffs, the Devils surprised a lot of people by even making it to the Cup Final. The Red Wings were the class of the NHL in that lockout-shortened season. They'd won thirty-three of their forty-eight games, scored 180 goals, and won the Presidents' Trophy for having the best regular season. Heading into the postseason, the Red Wings looked unstoppable.

Once the playoffs started, the Red Wings laid waste to the Western Conference. They went 12–2 as they crushed Dallas, San Jose, and Chicago on their way to the Cup Final. But the Devils players felt they could win.

"For the Cup Final, typically you fly into town for an away game the day before. We flew into Detroit two days before, to get prepared for game one. We woke up the first morning in Detroit and back then they had two newspapers, the *Detroit Free Press* and the *Detroit News*. On the front page of each respective sports section, there were five reporters giving their predictions for the series. Most predicted a sweep. One said that Jersey would get lucky, and the series would go to five games before the Red Wings would win the Cup. The last said that Detroit would win the Cup Final in *three* games because New Jersey would be so embarrassed, we would pack up and quit. That is what we woke up to our first morning in Detroit when we read the paper."

People in New Jersey don't intimidate easily, and certainly not the players on the Devils that year.

"We just laughed at it because we knew the Red Wings were highly favored. They had a potent offense and they had everything else going for them. People forget the year before we were in the top five in goals for. We were not just a neutral zone trap team; we had some offense that could produce because of what we did in the neutral zone. We could create turnovers and we had some speedsters who could take advantage of that and make things happen."

Did they ever. The Devils outscored and outhit the Red Wings in a four-game sweep. During the last two games in New Jersey, they beat up the Red Wings by a combined score of 10–4.

For McKay, the win was even sweeter considering the Montreal native had two Canadiens legends coaching the team in Jacques Lemaire and Larry Robinson.

"In 1995, it was cool to have them as our head coach and assistant coach."

Lemaire's coaching led to a funny example of why you should never judge a book by its cover.

"On that 1995 team, we had a few French guys like Claude Lemieux and Stéphane Richer and Marty Brodeur. Well, Jacques Lemaire did not say very much behind the bench. But Jacques and the francophone players would talk French to each other. When they were pissed off at someone on the team, they would all start talking French. I am from Montreal, and I went to French school, and I am bilingual. However, they had no idea about this. It took them a couple years to realize that I was fluent in French, and I understood every conversation they ever had. When they found out, they were not happy!"

Once the Devils were done celebrating with the fans in New Jersey, the players submitted the date they wanted to spend a day with the Stanley Cup. After years of semiorganized chaos over the summer, 1995 was the start of what we now know as the Stanley Cup tour.

"I had asked for a specific day in 1995. I ended up giving them two or three preferred dates for my day with the Cup. On the day they decided on, the Cup was supposed to fly in around nine in the morning, and then it was supposed to fly out the next day at the same time. Fog delayed the plane, and I didn't end up getting the Cup until later in the afternoon. I ended up having the Cup for only eighteen hours.

"I did a few events with the Cup, and then I took it to my house for a get-together. I promised that I would take the Cup to a downtown restaurant-bar in town, and I invited my friends."

The end of the night is where McKay's experience with the Cup took a surprise turn.

"After that was over, about six of us climbed into my boat and went to drive the Cup back to my house. We were all headed back for a party with the Cup and then we hit a big fog patch. We did not exactly get lost, but we couldn't see anything! And we didn't run aground, but we did get stuck a bit in the muddy bottom. While the Keeper of the Cup watched, two of us had to jump out of the boat to get us unstuck. We finally got to my house after a two-hour adventure, where it should have taken only twenty minutes.

"This was the first year they had a Cup Keeper around with the Stanley Cup. They used to ship the Cup from city to city, and you would have to go the airport and pick it up. We heard stories that the Cup got banged up and some of the previous teams got a little carried away with their celebrations. In 1995, from the time the Cup got there, until we drove him to the airport, the Cup Keeper never slept."

It wasn't all fun and games for McKay. He used the power of the Cup to raise money for a good cause.

"I did a fundraiser for youth hockey in Houghton. The plan was that I would take pictures with the Cup for two hours and I asked for a five-dollar donation. There was a big bucket there and all the money was going to local hockey. That two-hour session turned into three and a half hours. I left after two and a half hours, and people were still getting their photo with the Cup. I couldn't do it anymore and I had to take a break."

McKay is proud of hockey's history in Houghton. And when he had the Cup again in 2000, that history surprised even the Keeper of the Cup.

"In Houghton, Michigan, hockey is huge. In some ways, it is the birthplace of hockey. The Gibson Cup, which is still around, originated in Houghton, Michigan. It is one of the oldest North American hockey trophies in existence.

"Doc Gibson was a dentist from Houghton who loved hockey. He started a hockey league and at the time, there was a huge copper mine in Houghton, the biggest employer in the region, and the hockey league and the Gibson Cup provided an outlet for all the workers in their off time. Eventually, Gibson was inducted into the Hockey Hall of Fame in the builder category.

"There were all these people, some of them with money, with nothing to do. So, Doc Gibson built a rink, and he started a hockey league. There were teams from Sault Ste. Marie to Chicago to Pittsburgh and all over. The Gibson Cup was presented as a professional trophy not long after the Stanley Cup started to be awarded during the Challenge Cup era in the early 1900s.

"In 2000, I called around and someone had the Gibson Cup at home on their end table and they brought it around to my house. The Keeper of the Cup that year, Mike Bolt, was looking at me like I had two heads. I was trying to tell him the story of the Gibson Cup and he thought I had way too much to drink. Mike called back to the Hockey Hall of Fame and talked to his boss, who rambled on for five minutes about the Gibson Cup. He couldn't believe we were all in the same house together! I am probably the only person to have their picture taken with the Gibson Cup and the Stanley Cup."

Knowing that he had the Stanley Cup for a full twenty-four hours in 2000, McKay was determined to make the most of every minute.

"In 2000, my son was almost three years old, and he needed to take a nap. I went to his bed upstairs and laid in bed with him with the Stanley Cup. Riley never had his nap, but they have pictures of me taking a nap with the Cup in his bed. Because I only got the Cup for around eighteen hours in 1995, when we won the Cup in 2000, and they asked for our preferred dates, all I told them was, 'I will take it anytime in the summer, it doesn't matter what date, as long as I have it for two nights.' I had heard that certain guys had the Cup for two nights. One week later I got a phone call and they said, 'Okay, the Cup will be there in ten days.' It turned out I was one of the first stops in the summer of 2000.

"Around this time, I just had my house built in Houghton. They finished in June and were still working on a few parts and doing some painting as the Cup wrapped up. I told the contractor who built my house, 'Tell anyone who did anything on my house, they are welcome to come over and hang out with the Cup.' Houghton is a small town, so I knew a bunch of the workers already. The next night, I was thinking I would send out invitations for friends and family. Instead, I called my really good friends and told them, 'If you think you know someone that knows me well enough to come to my party, tell them to come on over.' It spread word of mouth and we ended up with a nice gathering at the house with the Cup.

"Because we had two nights, I was able to relax more and enjoy the Cup more. That second night, I sat around with my friends and the Cup in my kitchen for hours. We stayed there and hung out with the Cup until we had to drive the Keeper of the Cup to the airport. We stayed up all night and one of my buddies had to drive six hours to go to work, so he wasn't drinking.

"When it was time to go, we all piled in his van, and he drove the Keeper of the Cup to the airport. Then he came back to Houghton to drop us all off, and then drove at least five hours to a big meeting he had to attend."

For his second time winning the Cup, McKay knew from experience to do things differently.

"I hired a professional photographer. I realized that I didn't have enough good pictures the first time. We ended up having portraits done with the Cup in my basement. The photographer hung out with us and took pictures all night. I never thought about that in 1995. In 2000, I realized how quickly your time with the Cup goes and I just wanted to relax with it more. I had the time to take the Cup to my alma mater, Michigan Tech. My buddy was running a hockey school, and I brought the Cup for some more photos. After that, we went downtown to eat. Nothing was planned, we just thought we should stop and grab a bite to eat. We drove the Cup and parked on Main Street in Houghton. We parked and took the Cup with us and walked no more than thirty yards to go eat and people stopped dead in the street, staring at us with the Cup. We got into the bar and there was no more than five people there. By the time we left, there were at least two hundred! The Stanley Cup attracts people."

For McKay, spending some with the Cup with some of his closest friends is something he will never forget.

"When you have the Cup for as many hours as we do, when you have a quiet moment, you can really get a good look at it. When I did, I was amazed. Not only did I look at all the names, but I found some misspelled names on there as well."

Everyone who saw the Cup got a little emotional, some more than others.

"My friends and I were sitting around at two in the morning with the Stanley Cup on the table. It was a bit overwhelming. We were just staring at it for hours, enjoying the moment," said McKay.

Not that anyone could blame them. The Stanley Cup will do that to a person.

Thanks to Randy McKay and the New Jersey Devils, Houghton, Michigan, is not only known for its natural beauty, Lake Superior, Michigan Technological University, and its mining history. It is also known as a true-blue American hockey town. A town that proudly hosted the Stanley Cup twice. The memories of those two days are as important to the people of Houghton as they are to McKay.

Billy G. and Mr. C

Drafted in the first round of the 1989 draft, Bill Guerin joined the Devils after playing two years at Boston College. Like Daneyko and

McKay, Guerin was a part of the Devils team that suffered that painful loss to the Rangers in the 1994 playoffs.

Like McKay, going into the 1995 Stanley Cup Final against the Red Wings, Guerin remembers the popular opinion about their chances.

"Nobody gave us a chance and we were playing a different style of hockey, which was totally new to the NHL. Supposedly, we had no stars on our team. But we had a Hall of Fame goalie [Martin Brodeur], two Hall of Fame defensemen [Scott Niedermayer and Scott Stevens], a couple of fifty-goal scorers, and a couple forty-goal scorers."

The Massachusetts native had dedicated his life to hockey. Winning the Stanley Cup was great; getting to spend a day with it was even better. When the Devils proved everyone wrong, there was no doubt where Guerin wanted to spend his day with the Cup.

"I got the Cup back in my hometown of Wilbraham, Massachusetts. Wilbraham is about a twenty-minute drive outside of Springfield. For some reason, Pat Plunkett was our Keeper of the Cup for my day. The logistics of taking the Cup around North America and throughout Europe is too much for just one person. Phil Pritchard, the main Keeper of the Cup, had people like Pat to help. Otherwise, Phil would have burned out. I don't know why this happened, but Pat got out to my place a day early from somewhere else. So, I ended up having the Cup for two days.

"At the beginning, he tried to pull a prank and make me think he forgot the Cup. I didn't laugh. But Pat had a tough job. In the summer of 1995, Pat did almost all the players by himself. His boss, Phil Pritchard, organized the tour, and did all of the coaches, management, and team staff.

"We had a big party planned the next day, so the first day with the Cup was kind of quiet. I invited my old coach and some of my old teammates. We spent that first day with the Cup at my parents' house in Wilbraham. We had it sitting out on the old picnic table in the backyard. My buddies came over and that was the best because we were not dealing with a crowd, we just got to hang out with the Cup.

"My youth coach was a guy named Gary Dineen and he was my mentor. He was originally from Montreal and years before had played for the Springfield Kings. When he stopped playing, he ended up staying in Springfield. Gary comes in, and one of his former players has the Stanley Cup. When he walked in, he literally cried. I was able to spend time with the Cup and look at names. The guys who travel with the Cup, Pat, Phil Pritchard, and Mike Bolt, they know all the stories and details surrounding the Cup. They were able to give anyone a history lesson if they had a question. I enjoyed spending a quiet moment with the Cup. Because there are moments that you are with the Cup, and everything is so crazy you can't even think. Aside from those quiet moments, your time with the Cup is a blur."

Until he had his day with it, Guerin had no idea the effect the Stanley Cup would have on other people.

"The Stanley Cup is a magnet, and I didn't realize that until I had my day with it. Anywhere you go with the Cup, people are starstruck by it. Later in the evening we took the Cup to a local bar called O'Brien's Corner. A bunch of us walked in with the Cup. These two old guys were sitting in a booth, and I could hear them say, 'Huh, it looks like some softball team must have won a tournament.' I still laugh at that."

Fourteen years later, Guerin won the Stanley Cup as a grizzled veteran on the 2009 Penguins. (He later won it two more times as the assistant GM of the Penguins, in 2016 and 2017.)

"Winning the Stanley Cup a second time was a very different experience. The gap was so long. When I was twenty-four years old and won the Cup the first time with the Devils, I thought I was going to win every year. Then you don't, and the next thing you know fourteen years have gone by. The biggest thing was having my children there to celebrate with me. That was the best part of winning the Cup a second time. We were living in Long Island when I had my day with the Cup in 2009. Once again, I got really lucky. I got the Cup a little earlier than planned. The night before my actual day with the Cup, they showed up with the trophy. We didn't do much the first day. It just sat around the house. We were sitting in the kitchen with my wife, Kara, and the kids are running around, and we are taking all sorts of pictures. My wife's grandmother was there, my father-in-law, my mother, and one of Mom's friends. I had the Cup filled to the rim with ice and Bud Light beer. We just sat around, talking and telling stories, and the Stanley Cup was my beer cooler for the afternoon."

Guerin went out of his way to share with those people in his life who sacrificed so much for him.

"To have the kids there, celebrating with me in 2009, that meant everything. They were all old enough to understand what this meant. My wife and kids sacrificed a lot during my career. They picked up and moved every time that I got traded or signed somewhere new. They deserved to have their time with the Cup every bit as much as I did. Their life wasn't easy during my career. I know they thought it was neat to see their dad's name on the Cup. It made them understand why I do what I do and all the hard work that I had put into my career had paid off."

Guerin loves the fact that in the NHL, players get to spend a day with the league's championship trophy.

"Spending a day with the Stanley Cup is unique and you can't replicate it. If another sport tried to do it, it just wouldn't be the same. No other trophy carries the weight that the Stanley Cup does. My actual Cup Day in Long Island [in 2009], we went out that morning to the grocery store and the liquor store. Well, we took the Cup with us everywhere as we were shopping. I took my son and my father-in-law and the Cup guy, Mike Bolt, and the Cup and we all went and got a haircut. Then later that morning we were driving around town.

I had a Jeep, and we didn't have the top on. We were driving through Cold Spring Harbor on Long Island, and we were at a stop sign. This guy was walking on the sidewalk and he yelled over, 'Hey, is that the Stanley Cup?!'

"I said to him, 'Yeah!'

"He said, 'Wait!'

"He ran over and jumped on the back of the Jeep and just touched the Cup. He put his whole hand on the Cup for about a second. He looked at me and said, 'That is all I needed, thanks.' That was really cool.

"Later that day, we let our kids host a party with the Cup. This was an event that went from noon to three p.m. at the Shipwreck Tavern in Bayville, New York. It is a cool place for kids and our kids had invited all of their friends. When that was over, we went home and showered and changed. After that, we had rented out a beautiful restaurant on Huntington Harbor and we had a party that felt like a wedding. There were about two hundred fifty people there and we had an unreal time. It was great, but it takes a lot of out of you!"

Guerin is brutally honest about what his second experience with the Cup was like.

"I hate to say it, but yes, I did appreciate my day with the Cup more the second time that I had it. I had been a part of trades and playoff failures and you name it. You don't only have to be good; you have to be lucky, and you have to be healthy. So many things have to fall into place to win the Cup. Most guys go through their career without winning it.

"We don't get paid in the playoffs—winning the Stanley Cup isn't about the money. Just look at the reaction that guys have when they win. It doesn't matter if you are a first-line center or a seventh defenseman or a coach or a trainer: everybody sacrifices to win the Cup. It means that much to everyone on the team."

Guerin has many photos from his time with the Cup and his time as an executive in 2016 and 2017. But out of all of them, one rises to the top.

"My favorite photo of me with the Stanley Cup is in my office. It is of me and Randy McKay when we won the Cup in 1995 with the Devils. A friend of mine that was close to a lot of guys on the team that year owned a bar in New Jersey. This friend actually introduced me to my wife. The bar was called the Verona Inn, and when we won in 1995, that is where we brought the Cup as a team. I have a great picture of Randy and I filling the Cup up with beer from the tap behind the bar.

"I think I am one of the most fortunate people, ever. I didn't just win the Stanley Cup once; I won it four times. I have worked extremely hard and sacrificed a lot. Even having said all that, I still consider myself lucky to be in that position to have been able to have that many days with the Cup. It is a privilege to have your name on the Stanley Cup and spend a day with it.

"It was an even bigger privilege to spend a day with the Stanley Cup with my family and my friends. When someone looks at the Cup, they see my name on it. When I look at it, I see all of my family's names on it. Because there is no way I would have my name on the Cup without them. My NHL journey was tough on my family. I was traded four times, I was signed as a free agent three times, I played for eight teams, and they had to put up with all of it. Yes, I worked hard to play in the NHL for as long as I did, but they worked even harder keeping the family together. Nobody becomes a Stanley Cup champion by themselves. And it was their day with the Cup, just as much as it was my day."

CHAPTER 3

Potato Cannons and Dive Bars

1996 Colorado Avalanche
Scott Young and Mike Ricci

Born in Quebec, Made in Colorado

The 1996 Colorado Avalanche will always be able to trace their roots to the long-gone, but never-forgotten, World Hockey Association.

When the WHA folded, the Quebec Nordiques were one of four teams that joined the NHL. While the Oilers became a dynasty in the 1980s, the Nordiques never enjoyed that kind of success in the postseason. However, they did get good at drafting talented players.

The 1996 Colorado Avalanche team that ended up Stanley Cup champions was a long time in the making. Starting in the late 1980s, the then Quebec Nordiques began to build the foundation of what would become one of the best teams in the NHL from the mid-1990s to the early 2000s.

They drafted stars like Joe Sakic, Adam Foote, Adam Deadmarsh, and Milan Hejduk. The Avs were also helped by the Eric Lindros trade. In June 1991, the Nordiques drafted Lindros with the first-overall pick in the NHL entry draft and Lindros promptly refused to play for the Quebec Nordiques.

The Nordiques were far and away the worst team in the NHL at the time, having finished dead last in the standings the past two seasons. In 1991, a player refusing to go and play for the team he was drafted by was unheard-of.

Prior to the 1991 draft, Lindros made it very clear that he wasn't going to play for the Nordiques. So, when they drafted him, he went back to play for the Oshawa Generals and the Canadian National Team at the 1992 Winter Olympics.

The next year, in June 1992, the Nordiques were able to trade Lindros to the Philadelphia Flyers in exchange for Peter Forsberg, Mike Ricci, Ron Hextall, Steve Duchesne, Kerry Huffman, Chris Simon, $15 million in cash, and the Flyers' first-round draft picks in 1993 and 1994.

In fact, the Nordiques traded Lindros to the Flyers *and* the Rangers. It took arbitration to sort out the mess and a week later the Flyers had landed what was thought to be the best prospect to arrive in the NHL since Wayne Gretzky. A player so good, he was dubbed the Next One.

As the Nordiques moved to Colorado to become the Avalanche, Peter Forsberg emerged as one of the best players of his era.

Three months before the momentous Lindros deal, the Nordiques were able to trade troubled but talented defenseman Bryan Fogarty to the Pittsburgh Penguins in exchange for a veteran forward by the name of Scott Young. Sadly, Fogarty died in 2002.

Young, Ricci, and Forsberg teamed up with Sakic and Patrick Roy and turned the 1995–96 Avalanche team into a playoff juggernaut. The Avs beat the Canucks, the Blackhawks, and then they beat the number one seed in the NHL that year, the Red Wings, to get to the Cup Final. Once there, the Avs capped off their sweep of the Panthers by winning game four in triple overtime. The franchise that Eric Lindros once refused to play for was now a Stanley Cup winner.

The celebration, after such a tumultuous few seasons for the franchise, was all the more meaningful. Two players from distinctly diverse backgrounds had two vastly different Stanley Cup Day experiences.

Paying It Forward

The pride of Clinton, Massachusetts, Scott Young was no stranger to the Stanley Cup. Young already had his name inscribed on the Cup as a member the 1991 Pittsburgh Penguins. In 1991, the concept of a Stanley Cup tour was a long way from becoming a reality and Young barely saw the trophy after the Penguins won.

"In 1991, we did not get any time alone with the Cup," says Young. "If you were in Pittsburgh, you might have been able to grab the trophy for a bit. The Cup hung around Pittsburgh after we won, but it didn't go anywhere else."

By the spring of 1996, as a key member of the Avalanche Cup-winning team, Young had a very different experience.

Wearing white gloves, Phil Pritchard and Scott North brought the Stanley Cup onto the ice for the start of the celebrations. Afterwards, and like everyone else on the Avs that year, Young couldn't wait to get his day with the Cup.

"In 1996 after we won, General Manager Pierre Lacroix put a schedule together. He asked everyone to put in three or four weekends when you would like to have the Cup. A week after we submitted our requests for the schedule, I knew when I would get my day with the Cup."

To Young's surprise, he ended up on the top of the list.

"I was very fortunate; I was the first person to get the Cup that summer," says Young. "It was great, because the Stanley Cup victory was still fresh, and everybody was still celebrating. As opposed to getting the Cup at the end of the summer, when you are busy preparing for the next season."

Young was a veteran NHLer, but the thought of spending a day with the Stanley Cup with his family and friends made him feel like a kid again.

"I couldn't sleep the whole week before it arrived. I was so fired up. I could not calm down; I was looking forward to it so much. I ended up getting the Cup on June 27; it was a Thursday. At the time, I was living in Shrewsbury, Massachusetts, about a twenty-minute drive from my hometown of Clinton. Not only was the timing excellent, but I was also fortunate to get the Cup for two nights. I knew some guys only get the Cup for twenty-four hours. It arrived early in the afternoon on Thursday, and we picked up the Cup and the Keeper of the Cup in a limousine.

"The first thing we did, I brought the Cup to my golf course. I was a member at a private club, and we brought the Cup there and let some of the members drink out of it. After that, we brought the Cup to my house in Shrewsbury for a family party. It was just family there so they could get time with the Cup and take pictures and stuff like that. From there, I brought it to a bar in Clinton, the Crystal Café. The people at the bar kept calling me at my house in Shrewsbury and asking, 'Where are you? There is a line out the door!'

"The Crystal Café is a small place, but it is a place that has a lot of meaning to me. The reason I brought the Cup there is everyone involved with the bar was always incredibly supportive of me. They would travel to Quebec City when I played for the Nordiques. They would pack ten or eleven guys in an RV and drive to see me play. They drove out to Pittsburgh a bunch of times to see me play.

"Slip Tierney, the owner of the place, this little dive bar, was the driving force behind organizing these road trips to see me play and supporting me. I made sure to bring the Cup there first when it got to

Clinton. When we got there, there was a line out the door with a big sign welcoming me and the Stanley Cup. It is a horseshoe bar, and it was crowded when I walked in with the Cup. I was carrying the Cup through the crowd and Slip's back was to me. Being the owner, Slip sat in the same spot every day. I reached over his shoulder with the Cup, and I put it on the bar in front of Slip. He looked back and saw me, and he teared up and started crying. It was spectacular to see the emotion on his face."

Young was determined to share the Cup with his crew of friends from that tiny bar in Clinton, Massachusetts.

"I loved seeing the reaction from people when they saw the Cup. It is such a good feeling to be able to give back to these guys that followed me around and supported me."

Young was constantly amazed at how emotional people would get when they were near the Cup.

"Throughout the two days, I loved watching how excited people are when they are near the Cup. I am from the Boston area, and almost everyone when they got near the Cup would bend down and start looking for Bobby Orr's name and all the old Bruins. I would just stand back and smile. I loved it. Everybody was so happy and so into it. After they looked for Bobby Orr and the Bruins, they started looking for my name from the 1991 Penguins. It is great to see my name on there and know that it was going to go on there again. It is such an adrenalin rush and such a high to be with the Cup."

Other than booze, the only other thing he tried to put in the trophy was one of his kids, and that didn't go too well.

"We tried to put my one-year-old daughter in the Cup, and she started crying. For the most part, we drank a lot of beer and a lot of champagne out of the Cup. Even though we did a lot that first day with the Cup, I was too excited to feel tired or even a little hungover. Plus, I didn't have time to feel tired.

"The second day, we had a big event at the park in Clinton. We had people come up and get pictures with the Cup. There was a massive line of people waiting to get their moment with it. We spent almost five hours there, until everyone got their photo. We had people pay a little bit of money so we could donate it to the local hockey program in town. Later that night, we took the Cup to Turner Hall, where my dad was a member. This was a gymnastics club and bar in town. We had this big party with close to six hundred people. Phil and Pat had to leave for a moment and Phil told me, 'Hey, no drinking out of the Cup tonight!'

"He was thinking there is six hundred people there and it could get a little dangerous. As soon as he got a ride and left, I had everyone grab four bottles of champagne and filled up the Cup. When they returned to the hall there was this massive line. We were pouring the champagne from the Cup onto everybody. He just looked at me and started shaking his head. I said, 'Hey, I don't know if I am ever going to win this again, we got to take advantage of it!'

"The funny thing after all of that, Phil had to take the Stanley Cup to Pierre Lacroix's house for the next stop on the tour. He was leaving the next day around six in the morning. Phil called me later that morning after I woke up and he forgot everything. He forgot his wallet, his passport—you name it, he forgot it. He was begging me to go to FedEx and ship him his stuff. He said, 'Scott, you got to get this to me. I am going to the GM's house and Celine Dion will be singing there.'

"He got into Canada basically because he had the Cup with him. If he didn't have that, he never would have made it across the border. I ended up getting him his stuff, but he was in a panic."

When Young did have some quiet time, he was able to reflect and look back on some of the legends of the game he had played with up until that point in his career.

"I was lucky to play with so many talented players, beyond Mario

Lemieux and Joe Sakic. Peter Forsberg was great, Paul Coffey, Patrick Roy—I got to play with all of them. I feel truly fortunate to be able to play with all of those guys. I also got to play on World Cup teams and Olympic teams. On those teams, I got to play with Brett Hull and Mike Modano. Brett Hull could get a one-timer off from anywhere, and he could put it wherever he wanted. He was amazing; that is why he scored so many goals. When I talk to friends and they bring up some of the great names of the NHL, it hits me that I played with a lot of them. It is great to be able to say that and I played in a great era of hockey."

Like everyone else, Young took time to search out names on the Cup. There was only one team that interested him.

"I automatically went to the Bruins. I grew up watching Gerry Cheevers and Bobby Orr and Phil Esposito and all those guys and I looked them up on the Cup. The fact that my name is on the same trophy as those names, it is a surreal thing. It gives me the chills."

To this day, he's still not sure how to answer that standard question all champions get asked: "What does it feel like?" It is a really hard question; it isn't automatically euphoria when you win. There is a massive sense of relief when you win, because you have worked so hard and have gotten so far, and you did it.

"To not win would be devastating. I know someone has to lose. Fortunately, in the two finals I went to, I won both times. I can't imagine working that hard and going that far in the playoffs and not winning the Cup. When I watch the finals now, I always feel for the team that loses. As I got older, I was very happy to see certain guys win it and get their day with the Cup."

When it was finally time for the Cup to move on to the next stop on the tour, Young was a little sad.

"After I had my two days with the Cup, I didn't want anyone else to win it. I wanted to win it every year so I could always experience this," says Young.

Young was determined to squeeze every second out of his time with the Cup, right until the very last moment.

"My final night with the Cup, Phil and Pat were in bed, trying to get some sleep. My wife was asleep in our bed. I was trying to sneak up the stairs, while carrying the Cup," said Young.

"I wanted to sleep next to it before it left. It was dark and I didn't want to wake anybody up, and I tripped and dented the bottom of the Cup. Phil woke up the next day to polish it, but then he had to fix the dent first. He was a little irritated and asked me, 'Do you have a hammer?'

"And I could hear him as I was showering, banging away at the Cup in our living room, trying to fix the bottom. I didn't mean any disrespect; it was just a little fall in the dark at four in the morning after a lot of celebrating. It happens.

"Then I was thinking, this is his first weekend of the Cup tour. He had to do this all summer."

That is when Young realized how stressful the job must be.

"The Keeper of the Cup gets to know everybody on every stop along the way. Everyone would come up to him and tell him, 'What a cool job you have. You get to party all summer with the Cup!' Everyone that sees the Keeper of the Cup is so happy when he arrives."

Of course, after that first weekend, he was on thin ice.

In 2017, Scott Young was inducted into the USA Hockey Hall of Fame. When he looks back on his career and winning the Stanley Cup in 1996 with the Avs, there is one moment that still gives him a feeling of elation.

"When we won the Cup in Florida, we had the team celebration and the team photo on the ice. As we tried to skate off the ice, we went over to the gate and my dad opened it. I was stunned, I was thinking, *How did he get through this crowd and down to the gate to open it?*

More than anything, it is photos of Young with his dad and with his lifelong friends in the winning dressing room that bring him instant happiness.

"In the locker room after we won, there is a photo of me and my dad, holding the Cup up, over our heads. He has one hand on it, and I have one hand on it, and my mom is next to us. It is a great photo, and it still makes me smile to look at it," says Young.

Young also feels fortunate that he was, and remains, so close to his hometown friends.

Scott Young's dad and friend photobombing Joe Sakic *(left)* and Patrick Roy

"Every year one of my buddies will send me a picture of Joe Sakic and Patrick Roy after we won the Stanley Cup. Someone is taking their picture, but one of my buddies and my dad is in the background of the dressing room. My buddies and my dad photobombed Joe Sakic and Patrick Roy. My buddies were in the locker room celebrating with us and they were caught in the background of everyone. I will see photos from the winning dressing room, and I can pick them all out!"

Then again, that is what friends are for: a life filled with great memories. And best of all, memories that Scott Young was able to share with all of them.

Mom, Merlot, and Muskoka Nights

Mike Ricci will forever be known for two things. One, he is a Stanley Cup champion, and two, he was a part of the blockbuster Eric Lindros trade.

When the Quebec Nordiques moved to Colorado to become the Avalanche, the pieces received in the Lindros deal formed the founda-tion of one of the best teams in the NHL for the next decade.

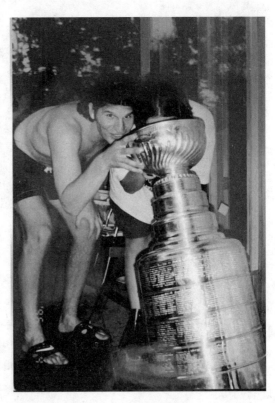

When asked about the Lindros trade, most people mention Peter Forsberg's name, but Ricci was a solid player, and he was coming off back-to-back twenty-goal seasons in Phila-delphia. Ricci's offensive production only got bet-ter when he was traded to the Nordiques. In each of his three seasons that Ricci played for the Nordiques, his numbers got better and better. That was until the franchise moved to Colorado and the team gathered to get ready for the 1995–96 season.

For Ricci, that season went from one disaster to another and resulted in his most frustrating year in the NHL. After only missing a handful of games in the previous four seasons, he played just sixty-two games in an injury-plagued season. To this day, Ricci is at a loss to explain what happened.

"The 1995–96 regular season was the worst personal year that I had in hockey," said Ricci. "I was put under anesthesia four times before the Christmas break. I had sinus surgery. Every sinus cavity was infected. I struggled moving to Colorado and I struggled adjusting to the altitude. It was so bad; surgery was the only option to fix my problem. Then I had a high ankle sprain. I missed a game and Mike Keane asked me, 'You practiced and played yesterday, what happened?' My foot had swelled up so much, it didn't fit in my skate. After that, I had a cyst in my mouth, and they had to take out my wisdom teeth to get the cyst removed. And to top it off, I herniated two discs in my back that year also. In the injury report it said back spasms. People would come up to me and tell me about this masseuse that could fix my back. I had a herniated disc. A masseuse wasn't going to fix anything. I had the herniated disc, and the first game back in the lineup we are in Toronto. I woke on the day of the game, and I had herniated the other one. I had missed training camp with my back problems, and I was so frustrated.

"The guys on the team calmed me down and said to me, 'Hey, just get ready for the playoffs. Don't worry about it.' I had only scored six goals that year and I was hurt all the time. I was ready to lose it. At one point I said to myself, 'What's next?'

"When we go to the playoffs, it was okay. We had so many veterans on that team, and they helped me through it. I felt like I owed my teammates a good playoff because I was so bad in the regular season. I had been missing practices, which I never liked."

Ricci more than made up for his lack of production in the regular season. He dressed for all twenty-two playoff games and scored six goals and had seventeen points during the Avs' run to becoming Stanley Cup champions. Ricci scored the game-winning goal in their opening game against the Red Wings in the Conference Final, and then he scored the game-winning goal in the opening game of the Cup Final against the Panthers.

It was a redemption story, not just for Ricci but for the whole franchise, only a few seasons after a move from Quebec, and that big turnover in players from the Lindros trade. And this was the same franchise that only won twenty games four years earlier.

Once the Cup parade in Denver was over, it was time to start planning for the summer tour.

"We had to submit dates when we wanted the Cup and there were rules attached. You get the Cup for two days on a weekday, but weekends, you could only get it for a day," says Ricci.

"I originally tried to get it for a weekday because I thought two days with the Cup would be great. But then my buddies and my family all said that they couldn't get the time off. So, I ended up grabbing it on a weekend day so everyone could enjoy it. I got the Cup on a Saturday morning in July, and it left Sunday afternoon the next day. In the end, it worked out for everybody because they were all able to come and enjoy the Cup."

When Ricci planned out his day with the Cup, he knew where he wanted to start the festivities.

"The Cup arrived at my mom's house in Scarborough. We had relatives there and neighbors all waiting for the Cup to arrive," says Ricci.

"It was a good way for my relatives and my nieces and nephews and my buddies to take some pictures with the Cup. As soon as it arrived, the Keeper of the Cup asked my mom if he could go in the house. He didn't want anyone to see him as he cleaned it and polished it before he brought it outside.

"He spent fifteen minutes cleaning the Cup and when he came out, it was shining, it was unbelievable. I still remember the looks on everyone's faces. I am from an Italian background and soccer is most people's first love. I didn't know how much the Stanley Cup meant to everybody until he walked out of the house with the Cup. Even my mom, she was so excited to have the Cup there," says Ricci.

"I know how much the Cup meant to me. I had been dreaming about and working towards it for years. I didn't know how important the Cup was to my family and friends, until they saw it. A lot of them had tears in their eyes. After people had their pictures taken with it, I had some time alone with the Cup. Our family, we had a lot of Montreal Canadiens fans, so we looked up their names. I do remember looking at Gordie Howe's name."

Once Ricci wrapped up everything at his mom's house, he took the Cup for a little road trip.

"We drove the Cup up to Haliburton, to my cottage," says Ricci. "Along the way we stopped for gas and something to eat. My buddy had grabbed three limos for the drive up there for all of us. We were on Highway 115 and there is a Harvey's hamburger restaurant beside the gas station. We stopped and grabbed some burgers and my cousin looked at me and said, 'Can you imagine if these people here ever found out what is in this limo?' We laughed about that. When he said it, he made it sound like there was millions of dollars of cash and gold in the limo. My cousins were emotional, just thinking about riding up to Haliburton with the Stanley Cup beside them.

"The outer shell of the cottage was done, but the inside wasn't even started yet. It was perfect for a party; we could abuse it and we wouldn't damage anything. I had a wraparound deck. I ended up bribing guys and getting more workers to finish the deck in time for the Cup party. They ended up working extra hours and brought extra guys in to get the deck finished. I told them, whoever works on the deck, if you get it done by Saturday, I will let you come down to take pictures with the Cup. It worked out well and we had a nice outdoor party. It turned out a lot of people ended up showing up at my cottage for the party. At one point, we took the Cup out on my bass boat for an hour and went fishing."

At that point, Ricci got a surprise visit.

"There were some people from Peterborough that had become good friends with my parents. Years before, my mom got into a car accident, and she needed some body work on her car. Our friend from Peterborough, he is an auto body specialist, and took Mom's car and had it ready to go in two days. Most auto body places would have taken weeks to do the same job. They had a floatplane, and they flew in from their place. At first, I didn't know what was going on. I thought it was some media trying to take photos of our party. I said, 'Who found out about the party and where I live?' Right away my mom says to me, 'No, that is the body shop guy from Peterborough. He said he knows the lake and he was going to land on it.'

"We had to move a few boats so he could tie up his plane. At that point, I hadn't met my neighbor yet. As the plane taxied to my place, I went over and introduced myself. I told him, 'Hey, man, this is going to get crazy and get loud.' He was great, he said not to worry about it. He came over later with his grandmother and we ended up becoming friends. My dock wasn't finished yet, so my neighbor anchored all his boats a hundred feet from the shore, so my friend could tie his floatplane to his dock.

"It was crazy times that night. My wife decided to do something and asked me, 'Do you think we could have people drink out of the Cup?' Every person there ended up drinking out of the Cup. We must have went through a case of champagne. We ran out of champagne, and we had to start pouring beer into the Cup. The music was blaring, they were playing 'We Are the Champions' from Queen, and everyone was drinking out of the Cup. Even my aunt was drinking out of the Cup; she just loved it! Every single person there took a drink. I don't even know if I went to bed that night.

"At one point, we brought out the potato cannon. A potato cannon is made from PVC pipe. You jam a potato into the top of the pipe, you stick hair spray in the bottom, and then you take a barbecue starter, and the potato shoots out. We had that thing launching a potato three hundred meters. I swear we hit a cottage across the lake. When we ran out of potatoes, we started launching watermelon rinds. It was a late night.

"What happened next, I still don't know how it happened, because this was 1996, but somebody's cell phone worked up there. A friend of ours had left the party to go play poker with some friends. A while later one of the cell phones in the cottage rings and this friend says, 'Look under the one table the pizza is on.' I told my cousin, 'Vinnie, go check it out, what did he leave us?'

"He left us a box of Cuban cigars and a case of red wine. I can't remember what kind of wine it was, but I know it wasn't the cheap stuff! We ended up having a bonfire, drinking the wine, and smoking the cigars. We sat up all night, and the Cup was sitting there with us.

"The Keeper of the Cup never leaves it. But at that point in the night, he looked at me and said, 'You guys are good?' I told him not to worry and go get some rest. When the Cup finally left the next day, *I* needed some rest. I loved having it for all of my family and friends, but in the end, I needed to get some sleep."

Ricci broke into the league in 1990 and played 1,099 games over his sixteen years in the NHL. He went to the playoffs seven more times after winning it all in 1996. He advanced no further than the

Conference Finals in 1997 with Colorado and then again in 2004 with the San Jose Sharks. Years later, Ricci still can't believe his name is on the Stanley Cup.

"I have a lot of good friends that haven't won a Cup. Because of that, I never talk about it. Privately, though, when I wake up, I sometimes think to myself, 'Thank God, I won a Cup.'

"I never remembered saying I wanted to score so many goals. The only thing I remember thinking is, *Man, I really want to win one of these.* I am blessed to have won a Cup, because I know a lot of good people who didn't. Every year I was in the NHL, and we made the playoffs, I always thought we had a chance to win the Stanley Cup. In the NHL, you fail more than you succeed. It is a tough thing to win."

Perhaps no one knows better than family just how hard it all is on a player. For Ricci, family is everything, and the best part of having a day with the Cup was seeing his mom spend time with it.

"When I think of my day with the Cup, I think of my mom. Having three boys and my father passing away, it wasn't always easy for her," said Ricci.

"Just being able to thank her for everything, that meant a lot to me. I spit out some words and thanked my mom for all of her sacrifice and everything that she did. And then to see her drink out of the Cup, that was special. My mom took time away from cooking to drink out of the Cup. She said, 'That's it, I am not cooking no more!' She just wanted to have a sip of champagne out of the Cup.

"For my mom and my aunt and my uncles, I made sure they had Dom Pérignon. Just watching my mom and my aunt and my uncles drink out of the Cup, that is my favorite memory of that day."

For Ricci, blood is thicker than water, and even thicker than the finest champagne, sipped from the Stanley Cup.

CHAPTER 4

Hockeytown Is Born

1997 and 1998 Detroit Red Wings
Mike Vernon, Mathieu Dandenault, and Anders Eriksson

Once upon a time, Detroit was home to Gordie Howe and the Production Line, and one of the greatest dynasties in NHL history. But by the 1970s, the Red Wings had fallen on tough times. Between the 1970–71 season and the 1982–83 season, the once-mighty Red Wings missed the playoffs a total of twelve times.

The next great chapter for the Wings began when Detroit drafted Steve Yzerman in 1983 and quickly made him the (then) youngest captain in league history at the age of twenty-one. Yzerman put together six one-hundred-point seasons and earned the right to be considered one of the great players in the history of the storied franchise. But even with Yzerman, it still took many hard years to turn things around.

The Red Wings still struggled in the postseason and Detroit could not be called *Hockeytown* until it won another Stanley Cup, something it hadn't done since 1955.

The long drought finally ended in 1997 when the Red Wings beat the Flyers in an emotional series with over forty years of weight on their backs. This championship was also a beginning: the Red Wings went on to be an elite team for the better part of the next decade.

A Very Canadian Affair

As with all top teams, there were many factors in their success. For Detroit, a big one was goaltending. After splitting time with Chris Osgood during the regular season, coach Scotty Bowman named Mike Vernon the starter prior to the start of the 1997 playoffs. Vernon would prove that Bowman made the right call, as he was rock solid during the Red Wings' twenty-game run to Stanley Cup glory.

Vernon was already a Cup champion, as he'd won it before with the Calgary Flames in 1989. Even though the concept of the Stanley Cup summer tour was still a few years away then, Vernon still managed to bring the Cup to his family home in Calgary that summer.

"We had a party at my parents' place with the Stanley Cup. All of the neighbors and other family friends showed up," said Vernon. "People would come by and take a picture with the Cup and have a drink. It felt like the whole South Calgary neighborhood stopped by at one point to take a picture with the Cup and say hi. Four of my former coaches from my youth hockey stopped by that day. My coach in tiny mites all the way up to midget showed up. Those coaches are still good family friends to this day."

By the time the Red Wings won the Cup in 1997, the full-blown summer tour extravaganza was in full swing. This time Vernon decided to spend the day with the Cup at his summer home.

"In 1997 I was at my summer home in Windermere, BC. Scott Oake of CBC Sports came out to Windemere to interview me at our cottage. I then took the Stanley Cup to the John Davidson golf tournament. All the foursomes would stop by and get a picture with the Cup. After that was over, I took it back to the house for some private family time. Then we took the Cup on the boat. I have a picture of my daughter, who was around two years old at the time, sitting in the Stanley Cup. She just fit!

"We had a party that night with a few friends by the lake. I ended up getting the Cup for a day and a half. Nothing too exciting happened during my time with the Cup. It didn't end up in a nightclub or in the bottom of a swimming pool. I wanted to spend time with people that I knew and friends from my childhood."

While he had the Cup, Vernon got to see his name engraved, along with the rest of the 1989 Flames.

"Seeing my name and seeing all of the other names on the Stanley Cup is really something. As you look at the Cup, you realize that there is not a lot of names on that trophy, because there are a lot of repeats. As you look at the Cup, it hits you. You think of the number of players in the NHL that have played, then how many names that are actually on the Cup. It is astounding how many good players are not on the

Cup. That is why the Stanley Cup is the holy grail and that it is why it is one of the most coveted trophies in sports.

"And also, you can drink out of it! That makes it one of the best trophies in the world. We drank some beer and some champagne out of the Cup that night. You have to drink out of the Cup. We are talking about Lord Stanley, and you have to respect him. By drinking out of it, you are honoring that trophy too and honoring what it stands for."

As much as Vernon loved being part of that Detroit team, sharing the Cup with family and friends stands out the most.

"When you win the Cup, you want to share it with your teammates in the dressing room afterwards. You usually have a team dinner with the Cup, and you get pictures with it then, and that is a great time. But the chance to take the Cup home and share the victory and to share that with your family and friends and people that you grew up with is important. All those people were a big part of my career, and they played a big role in getting me to the point of winning a Cup.

"I dreamed of winning the Stanley Cup since I was six or seven years old. I dreamed of hoisting the Cup over my head. There were a lot of years of training and working to get to that point where I did win, and I did get to hoist the Cup. To get to that point there were a lot of steps. I went from playing peewee to bantam to midget to junior and then on to the minors. Everything I did along the way all contributed to the success that I had in winning a Stanley Cup and in my career.

"Through it all, my family and my friends have always been there for me. They were there for me when I lost to Patrick Roy and the Canadiens in the 1986 Stanley Cup Final. They were there for me in 1994 when the Flames traded me to the Red Wings. No matter what, my family and friends always had my back and always supported me. That is why it meant so much to me to be able to share my day with the Stanley Cup with so many important people in my life. Without them, I wouldn't have become a Cup champion again in 1997."

When Vernon won the Cup for the first time, he immediately looked for the name of a player that meant a lot to him as a kid and a lot to him as an adult.

"When we won the Cup in 1989, the first name on the Cup that I looked for was Glenn Hall. He was my goalie coach for nine years and I have the utmost respect for that man and his career. He did a lot for the game of hockey. Glenn was my coach for nine years and we had a good rapport. He is also a legend of the game, and he holds the NHL goaltending record for starting five hundred two straight games, a record that will never be broken. The interactions that I have had with Glenn throughout my life, and those nine years when he was my coach—the man is a special man.

"I will tell you something interesting about Glenn Hall. He never came onto the ice once with me when he was my goalie coach. I saw him on the ice once, just skating. He was an amazing skater, he was fast. All of the players were shocked by how good of a skater he was. Glenn and I would talk, that's what we did. He helped me with the mental part of the game. He helped me to understand the game. Glenn would take unbelievable notes and we would sit after a game and talk. Or the next morning we would have a coffee and talk about the game. He would also talk to the shooters on the team. Glenn would tell them where to shoot on this or on that goalie. Glenn had a great insight on the game of hockey, and he was very instrumental in my success. That was one guy I looked for right away when I had the Cup to myself.

"You can take a paper and a pen and make a stencil of your name on the Cup. A lot of us did that and put it in a frame and hung it on the wall. You also get a miniature Stanley Cup to keep for yourself when you win it. I have two miniature Stanley Cups and a miniature Conn Smythe award. The original trophies stay in the Hall of Fame."

When thinking of those days, there is one photo that always makes Vernon smile.

"Both of my parents have passed away, so I love looking back at the picture of me with my parents and the Cup when I won the first time in 1989. We were in the backyard of our family home in Calgary. Those are the ones that I cherish."

Vernon adds, "I liked Bobby Orr as a kid, and I was a big Bruins fan growing up. I loved Orr and Gerry Cheevers and guys like that. It is kind of cool to think that my name is on the same trophy as all those great players."

A Part of Something Special

Anders Eriksson had come a long way since arriving in Detroit.

"When I came over from Sweden, I had a number of veteran players look after me," says Eriksson. "Nick Lidström was a mentor and Steve Yzerman was a big part too. Yzerman and Kris Draper trained with me over the summer, during my second offseason with the Red Wings. I stayed in Detroit that year and did my off-ice training with them. A lot of good people, who were superstars in the league, really cared and they really helped me. I remember Steve Yzerman telling me, 'I am going to take you under my wing.' I had a confused look on my face, and he said, 'Do you know what that means?'

"I looked at him. 'No, I have no idea, but it sounds good.' We laughed at that.

"If Steve Yzerman told me to jump, I would have only said, 'How high?' I was in awe of players like Yzerman and Lidström. Their work ethic and their dedication to the game of hockey was inspiring."

The hard work paid off. After watching the 1997 Cup run, Eriksson played sixty-six regular-season games in the 1997–98 season and then dressed for eighteen of the Red Wings' twenty-two playoff games, including all four of the Cup Final games in their sweep of the Washington Capitals. In that last game, he contributed an assist on Doug Brown's second goal of the game. Eriksson still cannot believe he was part of such a star-studded team.

"From that 1997–98 Red Wings team, I think there are nine Hall of Famers. It is ridiculous how good we were. I was twenty, going on twenty-one years old, when I came over from Sweden to play for the Red Wings. I didn't think much of how good the team was. Now, looking back, I have a different view of it. I truly realize how hard it is to win the Stanley Cup and how good of a team that I was on. It is incredible how many amazing NHL players never have been part of the opportunity of winning the Cup."

As the Cup toured Sweden in summer 1998, one of Eriksson's idols and mentors played a role in his time with the Cup.

"I was supposed to get the Cup for two days that summer. Nick [Lidström] had it and then he got sick. So I drove to his hometown, which is not too far away from me, and I picked it up. I ended up having the Cup for three days."

Home for Anders Eriksson is Bollnäs, Sweden.

"Esa Tikkanen's ex-wife lived in my hometown. I have known Esa since I was probably ten years old. We would always see him in Bollnäs every summer as he spent time with his family. Esa was back in Bollnäs when I arrived with the Cup and he started bragging that he had four of them, and I only had one!

"I rented out an old movie theater that was converted into a restaurant/bar. I invited all of my family, and I have a very large extended family. It turned into a two-day-long celebration. It was something that I will never forget. Bollnäs is three hours north of Stockholm, so in the summer, the sun is up to close to two in the morning.

"Like a lot of hockey players, I am from a small town. Slalom skiing was a big sport, ski jumping was a big sport, hockey was up there, but not number one—that was bandy. Bandy is played on ice on a surface the size of a soccer field with boards along the side. Instead of a corner kick like soccer, bandy has a corner pass into the high slot."

Sweden boasts a lot of great hockey talent, but when Eriksson was growing up, one rose above the rest.

"My older brother Jörgen was the person and the player that I wanted to be like. He was an amazing player and he played on the junior national team with [Nick] Lidström and [Mats] Sundin. They were all born in the same year as my brother, 1971. He ended up hurting his knee really bad in the early two thousands. But despite this, he still played in the Elite league for at least fifteen years. He was my idol. My second idol was Slava Fetisov, and not only did I get to play hockey with him, but I also won a Stanley Cup with him."

Eriksson is proud of his hometown, and he was even more proud to share his day with everyone.

"We have a square in Bollnäs and I put the Cup on the stage. Everyone in town came over and wanted to take pictures with the Cup. It was a huge celebration for the city of Bollnäs. It put the city's name on the map for hockey. In the province that Bollnäs is located in, we have produced some great athletes and some famous people. They once wrote a big article about it and said there must be something in the water. We have produced hockey players, bandy players, volleyball players, singers, models, and actors. Peter Stormare is a big actor in Sweden who grew up ten minutes from my hometown. Victoria Silvstedt, who was a *Playboy* Playmate of the Year, is from Bollnäs. She is now a successful businessperson. It is crazy to think from our province, how many people have been successful."

Winning the Cup allowed Eriksson to fulfill a promise.

"I took the Cup to the local pub. A longtime friend of mine ran the pub and I always said to him, 'If I ever win the Cup, I am going to bring it here.' I kept my promise and people to this day still talk about it."

Now that he is retired from the NHL, and has a family, Eriksson gets a kick out of his kids' reaction to his fame.

"My kids don't play hockey, but they skate, and they play other sports. I retired from the NHL before they were old enough to understand that I was a pro hockey player. Now that they are in school, their friends know who I am, and they ask for my autograph. My kids think that is weird. 'Dad, why are they asking for your autograph?' I always laugh when they say that!"

In fact, lots of kids in town knew Eriksson.

"I have tons of cousins. My dad is one of six kids, and my mom is one of five. It is almost like there is nothing else to do in Bollnäs but have kids! I am involved in a nonprofit organization that works with around a hundred and twenty kids teaching them about hockey. I am trying to pay it forward. Hockey is such a unique and amazing sport."

It is a big sport, but it is a small community. When he got his day with the Cup, sharing it with his hometown was the first thing on his mind.

"As excited as I was to have the Cup, it was great to see how everyone in the town was excited and happy. They were not just happy for me, but happy to see that the biggest trophy you can win in hockey, the Stanley Cup, was in their tiny town.

"Bollnäs is a tight-knit community, and it was a perfect place to grow up. Everything was accessible. Whether it was hockey, or downhill skiing or swimming, whatever you wanted to do, it was all ten minutes away.

"When I started playing hockey, I was pretty good. I played on the local senior team when I was young. Then I ended up going to a hockey academy put on by Modo in Örnsköldsvik. The Modo academy was mass-producing players. It takes a village to raise a child and it takes a village to raise a player that ends up in the NHL. A lot of people I had as coaches and friends and trainers all helped me. They drove me to practice and home again. They all played a role. When I brought the Cup back to Bollnäs, I got to see them and thank them for what they had done."

When he had a quiet moment, Eriksson did what every other player does when he has the Stanley Cup.

"I remember looking at all the names of the star players on the Cup and thinking, *This is never going to go away, they can't take my name off.* It was emotional thinking I was going to be on that trophy forever. It took a while for it to really sink in."

Third Time's the Charm

A versatile player who started as a forward but became a defenseman, Mathieu Dandenault carved out a solid NHL career for himself. Not only did he play close to nine hundred games, but he also got to spend a day with the Cup three separate times in his career.

"Even though I didn't dress for any playoff games in '97, I had been with the Red Wings since 1995 and so I had my day with the Cup like everyone else."

Dandenault was a young player who was just starting out in the NHL. He might not have dressed for any playoff games that year, but that didn't stop him from enjoying every second of his time with the Stanley Cup.

"I ended up with the Cup for almost forty-eight hours. I had a family get-together at my dad's place in Bromont, Quebec. I had everyone there and we were having a good time, then at eleven o'clock at night there were only five of us left with the Cup," says Dandenault.

"I got my turn with the Cup on a Monday night, the worst night of the week to have fun. We were trying to figure out what to do next when one of my buddies goes, 'I know, Bourbon Street! Monday is Industry Night!' Bourbon Street is a popular bar north of Montreal in the Laurentians. The five of us grabbed the Cup and piled into a car and started driving. We were driving way too fast, but we thought, *We have the Cup; it doesn't matter.* By the time we got there, there must have been close to three thousand people at Bourbon Street. We walked in with the Cup and started celebrating with everyone.

"Now, at the time, there were a lot of bikers there. There were a lot of Hells Angels who were there, partying the night we showed up. They walked to me and said, 'Can we touch the Cup?'

"I said, 'Oh, okay.'

"All the Hells Angels started passing the Cup to each other. I looked over at the Keeper of the Cup and he was freaking out. All the bikers ended up being very nice and we all had a big party. We stayed there until at least four in the morning, then drove back. I was twenty-one years old and that was my first experience with the Cup."

The Red Wings won again in 1998, and Dandenault had another day with the Cup.

"I had a family event with the Cup. Then I

Mathieu Dandenault with the legendary Gordie Howe

took the Cup to Quebec City. As a matter of fact, I took the Cup to Montreal and Quebec City that year. In Quebec City, I took the Cup to the two top bars in the city. I ended up having a great time and allowed everyone a chance to drink out of the Cup."

Getting the Cup to its next destination in Montreal led to a surprising roadside experience.

"The Cup had to leave early the next morning and it was supposed to be on a flight to bring it to Scotty Bowman. The Keeper of the Cup had to be on a flight out of Montreal at six in the morning. We were at the bar in Montreal until after three in the morning. The Keeper of the Cup looked at his watch and said, 'I have to go.'

"I have this big friend—he's over three hundred pounds and he's kind of rough-looking. He hopped in a Range Rover with the Cup and the Keeper and then they started driving to the airport. The next thing they know, they got pulled over by the cops.

"The police couldn't understand why this big, tough-looking guy was driving around in a Range Rover with the Stanley Cup in the middle of the night. Once they realized what was going on, the police on the scene called all of their cop buddies on the radio to let them know they were with the Cup.

"This is four in the morning and in 1998, nobody had cell phone cameras. Well, the cops went to the local mini-mart to buy those little throwaway cameras, so they could take a photo with the Stanley Cup. It all worked out and the Keeper of the Cup ended up making his flight."

By 2002, Dandenault was a key part of a Red Wings team that was unstoppable by the time they made it to the Cup Finals.

"In 2002, I played a much bigger role with the team than I did in 1997 and 1998 and logged a lot of ice time in the playoffs. Dave Lewis, one of our assistant coaches, really helped me as I became a defenseman in the NHL. He pulled me aside one day and said, 'Nick Lidström, he plays thirty minutes a game. There is sixty minutes in a game, and I can't play Nick for sixty minutes. That means if Nick isn't on the ice, you are on the ice. That means you are just as important as Nick. Because if you get scored on, we lose. Your role on this team is just as important, whether you play twelve minutes or twenty minutes.'

"As a player, that made me feel great and I always remember it. I still give that speech to this day when I am working with kids. No matter what, hockey is a team game. Because of that, the 2002 Cup win means more to me. I was older and more mature. I understood the importance of it more and we hadn't won in a few years. Of my three Cup wins, definitely 2002 meant the most to me."

Being a bit older meant that Dandenault had a different experience with the Cup that summer.

"By 2002, I was engaged to be married and I had quieted down a little bit. I ended up renting the top two floors of this big boat that cruised the St. Lawrence River. It was awesome and we were allowed to have a hundred and twenty-five guests with us. We started off in Old Montreal and we had a DJ and everything you needed to have a good party on the boat. It was only four hours. If I ever had a chance to do it again, I would have rented the boat for the entire day and into the night. I ended up talking to Vinny Lecavalier about it, and he did the same thing when he won the Cup in Tampa in 2004."

The boat cruise was nice, but seeing his name on the Cup twice was even nicer.

"It is always cool to see your name on the Cup. It is even cooler now, in the present day, when you are at different events with the Cup. You look at it, and you see your name, it is a great feeling. By 2002, I only had twenty-four hours with the Cup, so it goes by quickly. When I had it for two days, I was so tired at the end of it, I was happy to see the Cup leave! Every time you have the Cup, you build a relationship with the Keeper of the Cup. They are friendly and everything, but they get tired too."

Each time he had the Cup, Dandenault was reminded of all the people who helped him reach his goal.

"My parents were so important, and they sacrificed so much. Especially my mom and my stepdad. I lived with them full-time for a while and they took me to all of the tournaments. My younger brother ended up having to follow us around wherever we went, and he became a little rink rat. I remember at a ceremony where they retired my jersey in Sherbrooke, where I played junior, as my jersey went up to the rafters, it is my name, but is also everyone's name. Because they were all a part of the journey. They all came to see me play and they all helped me to be better."

When he was alone with the Cup, Dandenault wasted little time looking for the name of one player.

"When I had time with the Cup, I right away looked for Mario Lemieux's name. He was my idol growing up and it was great to see Lemieux's name and Gretzky's name on the Cup."

Dandenault still marvels at that 2002 team and the leadership of their captain, Steve Yzerman.

"That 2002 team was filled with Hall of Famers, but more than that, it was a team filled with patient players. Nobody ever panicked in a game or in a series. Younger teams panic in the final two minutes of a game, and they end up making a mistake.

"In the first round, we were down two–nothing to the Canucks and then our captain, Steve Yzerman, spoke to the team. He said, 'You know what, guys? I believe in our team. We lost the first two games at home, so what? They think they're great, but they have goals that have gone off a skate or gone off a shin pad. They have been lucky. I don't want us to change the system. If we just keep playing the way we can play, I think we are going to get a lucky bounce.'

"Sure enough, in game three, Nick Lidström scores on a shot from center ice. When he scored, we all looked at each other on the bench and said, 'Holy smokes, that is our lucky bounce!' We won that game and the next three games to beat Vancouver in six games. We all believed that we could win and that we could come back from any situation."

To Dandenault, the Red Wings had another secret weapon, Chris Chelios.

"He was a machine, unlike just about any player who ever played, and he would ride the bike in the sauna and then go out and perform every single night. Chelios would say, 'If I sleep more than five hours a night, I get stiff. So, I have to be out and about.'"

As happy as Dandenault was to win it all in 2002, he was happier to see two veteran teammates win it.

"In 2002, I was so happy to see Luc Robitaille and Steve Duchesne win a Cup for the first time. Luc was a star in Los Angeles and was on the Kings' top power-play unit. He came to Detroit and he eventually played on the fourth line in the playoffs. He did it for exactly one reason, to win a Cup, and he did. Luc made a sacrifice to win. I was also happy to see Dominik Hasek win. He was brought to Detroit to compete against Patrick Roy, and he did the job. To be fair, our Conference Final win over the Avs was like the Cup Final. When we lost game five at home, we had to go back to Colorado and Dominik shut them out in game six, and then he shut them out in game seven at Joe Louis Arena."

Like everyone else, Dandenault said everything tastes better when you drink it out of the Cup.

"I drank champagne and beer out of the Cup. Goodness knows how many lips have been on that Cup! I never did eat anything out of the Cup. When we took it to bars, we mainly drank beer. It is a cool feeling when you are standing on the bar, holding the Cup, and everyone is lined up for a turn to drink out of it. Before Tinder, it was a great way to meet people!"

The memory of winning the Cup is something Dandenault said will stay with him forever.

"Whatever happens and whatever people say, I was still there in Detroit, and I was still a part of the team. If you say that Wayne Gretzky is the greatest player ever, he only won the Stanley Cup four times. He played twenty seasons, but he didn't win the Cup twenty times. You need a team to win a Cup.

"Early in my career, when I was part of the back-to-back Cup teams in Detroit in 1997 and 1998, there were a few articles that came out. One of them said, 'How does Dandenault have two Cups, and Ray Bourque has none?' All I could to do was laugh. I was lucky to be drafted to a top team like the Red Wings. Bourque would finally win a Cup later on with the Avalanche.

"The one thing that you realize is that when you win a Cup, your teammates are like your family. Even if we have an event once a year, I will see some of the guys like Chelios and Draper and it feels just like it was yesterday. When you win a Cup together, there is a brotherhood that stays with you for the rest of your life.

"My name is on the Cup three times, and in 2002 it is extra special because I played every game. Winning the Stanley Cup as part of a team is the best feeling ever."

CHAPTER 5

Everything Is Bigger in Texas

1999 Dallas Stars
Mike Modano, Guy Carbonneau, and Craig Ludwig

Deep in the Heart of Texas

The 1999 Stanley Cup Finals between the Dallas Stars and the Buffalo Sabres was a brutal affair. Every inch of ice became a battleground and penalties were rare.

But championships take more than toughness. You don't win the Stanley Cup unless your best players are your best players. Captain Mike Modano assisted on all of the Stars' goals in game five and game six, and Eddie Belfour stopped seventy-six of seventy-seven shots before Brett Hull scored the series winner in overtime.

Not just overtime, but Hull scored the series winner in triple overtime with the now infamous foot-in-the-crease goal. While Sabres fans howled with protest, the Dallas Stars had won the Stanley Cup in six games. It was a tight series with little margin for error. Modano assisted on seven of the thirteen goals the Stars managed to score in the Cup Final.

For Mike Modano, his initial reaction was one of relief.

"We had to go through a lot to get through some of these teams to even get to the Cup Final. Hockey in general, prior to all of the rule changes that came later, it was a heavy, nasty, and dirty style of hockey in the playoffs. It felt like the hardest two months of my career."

As for the Cup-winning game itself, it was important to win sooner than later.

"The excitement leading up to game six, knowing that the Cup was in the building and ready to go—it gave us a ton of incentive to get it and end the series. We also felt as a team that we were getting depleted and getting hurt. We felt if the series did go to a game seven, we could have been in trouble."

Before Modano or anyone else on the Stars got their day with the Cup, the revered trophy had to first survive a series of team parties in Dallas.

"After we won on June 19, the Cup stayed in Dallas for a while. I didn't get my day with the Cup until late July or early August of that summer. The Cup was in Dallas for over two weeks after we won. There were a lot of requests from the owner, Tom Hicks, and other people on the team to have certain events. Most of the players felt after those two weeks we needed a break, because our livers were hurting!"

The Cup was finally returned to the Hall of Fame in Toronto and a tour schedule was organized with Phil Pritchard. By the time Modano got his official day with the Cup, things were much tamer.

"It was a simple day. There was nothing really crazy that happened. I had a barbecue with a lot of family and friends that came to town. We had a simple get-together at the house and then at night we went to a restaurant called Champs. One of the guys I knew really well in Minnesota was a manager at the Champs there and he moved to Dallas to open up the Champs in Texas. We kept in touch and when we won the Cup, I called him about having a party there and he was all for it.

"We had a little party, then we made a late-night pit stop at IHOP for a bite to eat. I had the Cup on the weekend and usually people pop into the IHOP after the bars close for a snack. When I walked in there with the Cup, we caught a lot of people off guard. There was a group of ten of us that walked in with the Cup and people in the restaurant couldn't believe it. I got home around two in the morning. Then Phil Pritchard was on the first flight out of Dallas later that morning. Considering what happened every night the first eight days after we won the Cup, my day with the Cup wasn't too crazy. There was nothing like the incident at Vinnie Paul's house!"

Like anyone who wins the Stanley Cup, Modano used it as a chalice for numerous beverages.

"When we went out with the team, we had a lot of Goldschläger and Jägermeister out of the Cup. We had some guys on our team that could go really hard, and they knew how to step it up when they wanted to have a good time. They were hard to keep up with!"

And like so many other champions, Modano used his time with the Cup to look it over and search out the names of his heroes.

"When I got the Cup at my house, I looked for Bobby Orr's name and Gordie [Howe] and Wayne Gretzky and certainly Mario Lemieux. I searched out Steve Yzerman as well. Then it hit me: my name is going to be engraved with these guys on this Cup. It made me realize that

I am part of something that has been going on for a hundred years. My name was now on the same trophy as some of the most iconic names in the sport.

"Early in the morning, when Phil Pritchard arrived with the Stanley Cup at my house, my parents and I had a nice quiet moment with the Cup. We were in the kitchen, and we all took a moment and stared at it in awe. I couldn't believe the Cup was in my house. It hits you: we really did it, we really pulled this off and won the Stanley Cup. It was amazing. I never thought in a million years that I would get to that point."

As much as Modano loved celebrating with his teammates, he appreciated the quiet moments he had alone.

"Being away from all the noise that comes with a team party, and you are just sitting there with the Cup and reflecting on the journey. I was thinking about what I had gone through and what we all had gone through the two months it takes to win. We were banged up and not feeling well physically and mentally. We got to a point of exhaustion that I never thought my body could go through and survive. Winning the Cup tests you in every aspect of the game."

Modano's only regret is that he wishes he had more photos from that day.

"Back in 1999, cell phones weren't cameras. That stinks because we could have got a lot of great photos and videos that day. Back then, people didn't carry around cameras for the hell of it. Looking back on my day, I should have hired someone to follow us around and take pictures."

But the memories last, regardless, and Modano still feels lucky that he was part of that 1999 Stars team.

"We had a nucleus of guys on that team that were young, and we all went through a lot of the same growing pains at the start of our career. I think of Jere Lehtinen, Darryl Sydor, Ed Belfour of course, Derian Hatcher, and Richard Matvichuk. A lot of these guys go back to my draft year in Minnesota. I thought of Brett Hull as well. We all felt it was our time and it was going to happen. If it hadn't, it may never have. We were the perfect team put together for that Cup run in 1999.

"Looking back, I think the thing that stood out was having the chance to share it with neighbors and their kids. I took it around to children's hospitals and visiting the kids with the Cup was great. I just wanted to have the people who hung with us through thick and thin and with me individually to see it and tell them how much they all meant to me.

"Being able to share the Stanley Cup with lots of family and friends at our own party was a memory I will have forever. Winning the Stanley Cup isn't a me experience, it is a we experience. As in, we did it and I wanted to thank as many people as possible."

Mission accomplished for Modano, as he spent his entire day sharing the Stanley Cup with family, friends, kids in a hospital, and late-night patrons at a local International House of Pancakes.

Keeping His Promise

It was quite the team. Modano was part of that young group that came up together, but a championship requires all kinds of players. Guy Carbonneau's name was already on the Cup twice before he arrived in Dallas. One of the best defensive centers of his era, Carbonneau was a big part of the 1986 and the 1993 Montreal Canadiens teams that won it all.

While official summer tours didn't begin until the mid-1990s, Carbonneau was able to take the Cup to his hometown in Sept-Îles, Quebec, in the summer of 1986.

"Along with the city, we organized a little celebration and people were able to take a picture with the Cup," says Carbonneau. "My family has a summer place, just outside of town, right on the St. Lawrence River. We had a party there with the Cup with a bunch of family and friends. It was fun, and the first Cup you win is always special. It was the first one for me and the first for the city. It was pretty amazing that day.

"Canadiens fans in Montreal are excited through the season and especially when the team is doing well. But once you get into the play-offs, everything escalates. Every series that you win, you gain popularity, and you gain fans. People start to believe in you a little bit more."

One of Carbonneau's favorite photos is of Denis Savard's face when the Canadiens won in 1993.

"In 1993, I was one of the veterans on the team. Nobody was happier to touch the Cup than Denis Savard. He came to Montreal, then he got injured, then he wasn't playing. Handing him the Cup when we won was fun, seeing his face and his eyes when he grabbed it. Everyone who touches it for the first time, or they see it for the first time on the ice, it is a special moment. Because I was a veteran, I had a much better understanding of what goes into winning a Stanley Cup. So many good teams and so many great players never win a Cup. There are Hall of Fame players who hold all of these records and they have

never won a Cup. I faced Denis Savard many times when he played for the Chicago Blackhawks. I knew how good he was and how respected he was around the NHL for his skills.

"In 1986, I was a young player, and it was that moment for me and my family. My dad was there, my mom was there, and my brother was there in the room with us and the Cup. My dad was a fan, but he never really talked hockey with me. Then to see him with the Cup and for him to see his son finally do it, it was a fun moment.

"After we won the Cup in 1993, I brought it back to Chicoutimi, Quebec, where I played junior hockey. It was a different experience than my hometown. But I figured that Sept-Îles already had their shot with the Cup, so I brought it to Chicoutimi. I played four years of junior there and for a long time I used to live there in the summer. It was fun to bring it back there. Whoever started that tradition of players getting the day with the Cup is a genius. That is one thing that makes hockey and the NHL special. I have never heard stories about that from other sports leagues. You are able to take some time to enjoy the Stanley Cup with your family and friends. Kudos to the NHL for letting us do it when we win."

Like all players, Carbonneau was excited to see his name on the Cup.

"The first time I had the Cup, I couldn't wait to see my name on it. When I got inducted in the Hockey Hall of Fame [in 2019], I had all my family there and a bunch of my friends. After we played the alumni game, we went to a bar. They surprised me and had the Stanley Cup there. I had my youngest daughter with me in the dressing room in 1993, but she never really had the chance to get a good look at the Cup. It was a fun experience to go through the Cup and show my nieces and nephews that never saw me play and show them my name."

As a veteran on the 1999 Stars team, Carbonneau knew what it took to win, and what it would mean for his teammates. But everyone has their own unique burdens to bear. The 1999 playoffs were an emotional time in Carbonneau's life.

"During our series against Edmonton, my dad passed away." Carbonneau left the team to attend the funeral and then rejoined the other players. "I had made a promise to myself that if I won the Cup, I would put it on his tomb, in Sept-Îles. So, when we won, I went back home, and that is exactly what I did."

Before Carbonneau fulfilled his promise, he celebrated in Dallas along with the rest of his teammates.

"The parties after we won the Cup were the fun part of being in Dallas. When I got there in 1995, Bob Gainey was starting to build that team. Every year we got better. When we won, that was the first time anything like that had happened in Dallas or Texas. The Cowboys had won championships, but the Mavericks hadn't won anything yet and neither had the Texas Rangers.

"There were a lot of guys on that team who had never had a chance to win it before. It felt great, going through the building process over three or four years, and then to finally win it all. The players were really happy, the team was really happy, and the fans were really happy.

"We had team parties at Mr. Hicks's [Stars owner] house, we also had parties at Vinnie Paul's house. We had parties everywhere!"

Carbonneau takes partial responsibility for the Cup ending up in Vinnie Paul's pool.

"I admit, it was a bit of bad throw on my part, and it was a bad catch by Craig Ludwig when I threw up the Cup and he dropped it into the pool. A lot of people blame me for that, but there were not a lot of guys that would have done any better. But the Cup doesn't float, that's for sure."

The Cup has endured a lot over the years. Some incidents are accidental, some not.

"One of the years I won the Cup, a bunch of us took the bottom off and wrote our names with a nail inside. Then we put the bottom back on. Let's face it, Phil Pritchard has seen just about it all over the years. Then again, when you bring the Cup to a party with a hundred people, things happen. As long as you don't destroy it, that is all that matters."

Carbonneau said that while fans see the celebrations on the ice after a team wins the Stanley Cup, they don't really understand how hard it is.

"I played nineteen years in the NHL, and I didn't miss the playoffs very much. It didn't matter if it was one round or four rounds of the playoffs, you are always beat up at the end. Obviously, the deeper you go in the playoffs, the tougher it gets.

"I was lucky as a player; I went to the Stanley Cup Final five times, and I won it three times. People keep asking me, 'Which Cup is the most interesting?' It is always the first one, in 1986. When the buzzer went at the end of the final game, the first thing through your mind is all the memories you have: all the practices and all the games and all the tournaments. I could remember all of the trips I had to take with my mom and my dad. That moment after we won in 1986 and all of those memories is something that I will never forget."

At the age of thirty-nine, Guy Carbonneau was able to raise the Stanley Cup over his head one last time. Five years earlier, he joined a Dallas Stars team that won only twenty-six games. Three years later, they lost in the Conference Finals to the Detroit Red Wings. The next year, on a stifling-hot night in Buffalo, the ageless Carbonneau played a remarkable fifty shifts as the Stars beat the Sabres in triple overtime. Considered one of the greatest defensive forwards of his era, Carbonneau didn't play the game for the glory. He played to help his team win, to see his name etched on the Stanley Cup, and to make his dad proud. And that was something he did many times in his career.

The Life of the Party

Guy Carbonneau wasn't the only former champion on the 1999 Dallas roster. Craig Ludwig, the pride of Wisconsin, also won with Carbonneau in 1986, and he had a much different summer afterwards.

"We partied for three or four days to celebrate. Larry Robinson and his business partner owned a garage and I had bought a Corvette from them. It is at least twelve hundred miles to drive from Montreal to my hometown of Eagle River, Wisconsin. I took my Montreal Canadiens gear bag, and I propped it up on the passenger seat. I probably drove at least ninety miles an hour the whole way home. I got stopped by the police three times. Lucky for me, I was still driving in Canada. Having that Montreal Canadiens gear bag in the passenger seat got me out of a ticket all three times! They all said, 'Have a good time and thanks for the Cup.'"

Growing up in Eagle River kept Ludwig grounded.

"I went to college in North Dakota for three years. During that time, we won three national championships. My buddies were a little different. They would just say, 'Good for you, what are we going to do tonight?'" said Ludwig.

"When I won the Cup in 1986 in Montreal, that was a bit of a bigger deal in my hometown." The Cup wouldn't go on its summer tour until 1995, however. "Prior to bringing the Cup home in 1999, the biggest thing that I brought to my hometown from Montreal was Bloody Caesars. In Wisconsin, they had never heard of Caesars before, and neither had I. I brought back two cases of Clamato juice. Nobody knew what it was. However, people in Wisconsin love their Bloody Marys. Once they got a taste, I had calls from people asking how they could get more. That was my contribution to Wisconsin after winning the Cup in Montreal—the Bloody Caesar!"

By the late 1990s, Ludwig was near the end of his NHL career. At the start of the 1998–99 season, he wondered if he would even play that year.

"I was planning on hanging up my skates the year before, but my wife at the time encouraged me to play one more year. I stuck it out for the season, and everything fell into place. When we won in 1999, it was thirteen years after I won it with Montreal. I knew that Michael Jordan and John Elway both retired after they won a championship, and they had these parades and celebrations. My thought was, *Well, I am going to do the same thing.* I'm still waiting for the celebration and the parade!

"I felt it was the right time to retire after we won in 1999. Things were getting faster in the NHL, and I was headed in the opposite direction. I was very happy by the end, because I never had any intention of playing pro hockey when I was young. I looked at every year in the NHL as being fortunate. When we won in Buffalo in 1999, and everyone was sitting in the dressing room and smoking the cigars and all that, I said to the trainers, 'Can you get me a case of beer?' I kicked them out of the training room, and I brought in my wife at the time and my kids into the room. I looked at them, and she looked at me, and right away she said, 'You're done, aren't you?' I said yes and then I told my kids I was done playing in the NHL.

"The winter after that season, I was snowmobiling in Wisconsin with six of my friends. This was early in the afternoon on a very cold January day, and I got a call from Bob Gainey. My friends are loud, so I had to walk outside to hear him, and I didn't take my jacket with me because I figured it was going to be a short conversation.

"Bob asked me if I was interested in coaching. I told him I would get back to him. Bob Gainey is my Scotty Bowman; I have so much respect for him. I called him back in a week and told him that I would do it. Then Bob said, 'Why don't you grab your equipment and bring it with you?' I was confused. As a coach I was only going to bring my skates, a stick, and my gloves. Then he asked me to come back and play that next year. I finally had to tell him that I hadn't skated competitively since we won the Cup. And my twins were just entering high school. I told him, 'Bob, I don't care about embarrassing myself, but I know my kids are going to have to go to school and get teased because someone danced around me and scored a goal.'

"The next thing I knew, I was with our minor league team in Kalamazoo, Michigan, watching the Stars go back to the finals. Then I was thinking, *I blew it! I could have been there.* But working as a coach allowed me to stay in the game. I went from Kalamazoo to Utah when the team moved there. Then I came back to Dallas to work as a coach. From there I worked a pro scout and then the TV thing kicked in. Bob Gainey always gave me an opportunity to somehow hang around the game."

While it is well known about the night the Stanley Cup ended up in Vinnie Paul's pool, Ludwig admits he started it all.

"To be honest, I was probably initiating it and told Carbo to throw me the Cup. I had taken the Cup to a friend's bar in Dallas called the Big Apple. After the Cup bounced around a few bars, it ended up at Vinnie Paul's house. Vinnie was that guy who was always around the team, and he loved hockey. The whole band liked hockey."

Vinnie and his heavy metal band, Pantera, wrote a Dallas Stars fight song called "Puck Off."

"I called Vinnie up before the playoffs and told him that we needed some music. Within twenty-four hours, Vinnie and Dime [the late Dimebag Darrell] wrote that song and they are still using it. To us, Vinnie Paul was like one of our teammates. That year, Vinnie was a big part of our team, and I was with him all the time that year. After we swept the Oilers in the first round, we had a few days off before the beginning of the second round. Vinnie had called me up two days after we beat the Oilers and said, 'Hey, be at the airport at six, tomor-

Vinnie Paul of Pantera *(left)* and Craig Ludwig

row morning.' Vinnie knew we didn't have practice for a few days. He said, 'You're coming with us, you are coming with us.'

"I finally said, 'Dude, what is going on?'

"Vinnie said, 'Well, we [Pantera] are going to Mexico City, and we are opening up for Metallica. I know you are a big Metallica fan, and you are coming with us. I already talked to [James] Hetfield and told him you're coming.'

"I didn't believe him at first. Now, this was something like two in the morning when he called, and I hung up the phone. Five minutes later I called him back and said, 'What time is it again?'

"He said, 'We leave at six.'

"I hopped on a plane and flew to Mexico City with Pantera and spent a couple of days there. I never told anyone that story until a few years ago. Here we are, in the middle of the Stanley Cup playoffs, and I decided to get on a plane with a heavy metal band and go to Mexico City. It all worked out okay and we came back, and I got ready to face the Blues in the second round."

The series against the Blues led to one of the funnier moments of the 1999 playoffs.

"The song that Vinnie Paul wrote for us was on a CD. We clinched our second-round series against the Blues in game six in St. Louis. I don't remember dates and teams and things like that. But I do remember that night before game six, before we beat the Blues. I remember because the trainers forgot to pack the song before we left Dallas. We played that song before warm-up all the time. When I realized we didn't have the song, I called Vinnie and asked him to courier another CD to us. I figured out they forgot to bring it the day before at our skate. That song was a big part of our routine and we had to have it. The song got there, just in the nick of time. Hitch [coach Ken Hitchcock] came in just before we were supposed to go on the ice for game six. Hitch was always calling me into his office to talk to me about something. He looked at me and said, 'What is going on?'

"I told him, and he said, 'I don't care.'

"I said to him, 'Hitch, you don't understand, we are not going out there until the song gets here.' Hitch gave his pregame speech, and the song still wasn't there. It had just arrived at the building. Because of all this, we were late to get on the ice, because we had to hear that song. I swear, we heard three or four notes of the song, and we were good to go."

The timing of that infamous party at Vinnie Paul's house after the Stars won the Cup could not have been worse.

"Unfortunately, that party at Vinnie's house was the night before the Stanley Cup parade. My parents were in town for it. I was woken up around four in the morning at a Burger King. A worker said, 'Sir, you can't sleep here.'

"I had stopped from Vinnie's house on the way to my house. We were all supposed to meet at our practice rink to get ready for the parade. They had buses for players and one for families and wives. I was holding everything up because I wasn't there on time. My dad was already on one of the buses and I got on that bus and my dad gave me that look, he was not very happy with me!"

Fortunately, it all worked out. Later, Ludwig got his day with the Cup at the perfect time.

"I got the Stanley Cup for the Fourth of July. Mr. Hicks, the owner, was supposed to get the Cup then, but something happened, and he had to reschedule. After that happened, they called me and asked if I wanted to take it. I immediately said yes, and I called home. When I called them, they took an eighteen-wheeler and built a big float on a trailer. My dad invited all my ex-coaches and even the referees and linesmen that I had all the way up to college hockey to be a part of the parade. I got on the plane with the guy with the Cup from Dallas and we landed on July 3 in a town called Rhinelander, Wisconsin. Rhinelander is about twenty-five miles from Eagle River, and it is the only real airport close to my hometown. I said to the guy with the Cup,

'There's a bar in Rhinelander that I played baseball for. Is it okay if we stop by and take the Cup in?' It was a father and son who ran it, and they were big fans of mine. He said sure and we took the Cup to the bar.

"What I didn't realize is that in Rhinelander, they celebrate the Fourth of July starting on the third. Rhinelander always has this fireworks show the night of the third and then the party spills over into the early hours of the Fourth of July. A lot of the communities in that part of Wisconsin like to make the Fourth of July a two-day party. I don't know why they do it; that's just what they do there.

"We walked into the bar with the Cup, and it was packed. Nobody knew I was coming, not even the bar owners. I just wanted to surprise him. We ended up staying there a long time. It was ten in the morning, and it was packed with locals getting ready for their parade. I was behind the bar at one point and this girl came up to me and said, 'What is going on here? There is all this noise and there is some kind of trophy in here. Why is there this big celebration?' She had no idea what was going on.

"We eventually made our way up north to Eagle River. The Cup was in a parade, and in my area of Wisconsin, there is a chain of twenty-eight lakes. A friend of mine had a fifty-foot houseboat and we had fifty people on it along with the Cup. The boat almost flipped over at one point, but thankfully it didn't. After a good day and a half with the Cup, I got a call before I was about take it to the airport. They said, 'Hey, do you want the Cup for a couple more days?' The Cup guy was sitting next to me and the person talking said, 'Something got delayed again and if you want the Cup for a couple more days, it is all yours.' I was ready for the Cup to go to the next stop, but then I thought about it and said, 'Yeah, you know what, I will take it to my bar.'

"I co-owned this bar, about ninety miles away. The Cup guy kind of looked at me and said, 'Not that biker bar?' I covered up the phone and told him, 'It will be okay.' He started to turn white, just thinking about it. The bar was called Legalized Insanity, and we had the Cup for a couple of days there. That was a whole different level of crazy because of the kind of bar that it was. It was a dive bar when we got it and I wanted it to stay that way. We had a biker gang in the area called Satan's Pride. They walked in and the Stanley Cup was sitting there on the pool table. The bikers walked in and looked at the Cup like there was a force field around it. I said to them, 'Go over and pick it up. Take some pictures and drink some beer out of it. Have a good time with it.' The Keeper of the Cup was freaking out.

"Within an hour, the bikers were standing up on the bar and had the Cup over their head. Now, this bar had these wooden beams, and they were low from the ceiling. Every time the bikers lifted the Cup over their heads, they banged it off these wooden beams.

"A couple of hours later, I took the Cup outside and placed it on a table. Then I looked at the Keeper of the Cup and said to him, 'Where is the Cup at?'

"He looked at me. 'Ah, we will find it later!'

"You have to understand, the Keepers of the Cup end up becoming exhausted while watching over the Stanley Cup and the players. Eventually they need some rest so they can function. We stayed at my buddy's house who I owned the bar with. We got up the next morning and the Keeper looked at me and says, 'Where's the Cup?'

"'I don't know!'

"I had only got to sleep a few hours earlier and we were leaving that day to go to the airport. Now we were in a little bit of a panic because the Cup wasn't in the bar, and it wasn't in the house. We were retracing our steps to figure out the mystery. Well, one of the kids goes, 'What's that?'

"We looked out of the kitchen window at the hot tub and the Cup was in the bottom.

"As I got into my truck, the Cup guy asked me, 'Hey, can I borrow your phone?' He called the trainer with the Dallas Stars [Greg Smith]. 'Smitty, I get in tonight. Can I get into the training room?'

"Smitty goes, 'What do you need?'

"He said, 'I need to tear this Cup apart and fix it! He needed to wash it up and take out any little dents there might have been in it.'"

Considering how long Ludwig had the Cup that summer, it isn't shocking that it needed some repairs.

"I ended up having the Cup for almost four days in July of 1999. To this day, in my area of Wisconsin, they still talk about it. I was very fortunate to have the Cup at the perfect time. Our town shuts down for the Fourth of July and everything is outdoors. At the same time, all the tourists come in from the lake to watch our little Fourth of July parade. At the end of the parade, I stood on the back of the flatbed they made for us for at least three hours. We set it up so you could take a picture of the Stanley Cup and get an autograph.

"We have an organization called the Eagle River Recreation Association, the ERRA. We charged everyone five dollars a photo with the Cup, and all the money went to the ERRA. It helped raise some money for the local rink that we all skated at as kids. We strategically set up the flatbed across from this bar and they kept bringing us pitchers of old-fashioneds all day long. The weather was great, and it really was a perfect day for me and my parents and all the people that I grew up with and played hockey with."

For a small town in Wisconsin, you couldn't have written it up any better. Ludwig is enormously proud of where he comes from.

"I was so proud to take the Cup back to my hometown. I didn't have that opportunity in 1986, because the policy of touring the summer with the Cup wasn't around. When they started doing it, I remember thinking, *Man, that would have been cool if I were able to take the Cup back to Wisconsin.* When you go back home, those are all the people that supported you. They came to the games when you were younger;

the dads were coaches and families drove their cars to outdoor rinks. Every time I would come home in the summer, they were all the first ones to ask me what happened during the season. I don't remember exact moments in games, and they would ask me specific questions about hitting this guy or a game that we won. I would sit there at the bar and listen to them and politely try to answer every question.

"It is very touristy in the summer and there are a lot of people from Illinois who come there for vacation. That means there are a lot of Chicago Blackhawks fans there. It doesn't take long for them to realize that I play in the NHL and usually the next time I see them, they are wearing a Chicago jersey. It is funny in my hometown to see how many people went from wearing Montreal Canadiens jerseys to Dallas Stars jerseys. Now that I don't play anymore, they feel okay to wear both of them.

"Everyone in my hometown felt like a part of my career and they were a part of it. Where I grew up, we all played baseball, football, and hockey. When I was growing up and playing high school hockey, our little town would pack our local arena for games. Some of the guys from our town went on to play pro in Europe. I was just lucky enough to play at a dominant college program at North Dakota.

"It was more important to me that all those people in Eagle River got to spend time with the Cup and be a part of the parade. And having the parade on the same day in Eagle River took the burden off me of having everyone come over to my place. The whole town was at the parade for the Fourth of July, so they were all able to celebrate with the Cup. My really close friends all came over to the house for a more private celebration. They stayed with me for two days and most of them followed me to the other bar for the second half of the party. Yes, it is our day with the Cup, but it is really *their* day with the Cup."

Craig Ludwig might be the only Stanley Cup champion who never spent much time actually looking at the trophy.

"I never had a quiet moment with the Cup. I didn't have one time when I was with the Cup by myself. I had people with me twenty-four seven. I mean, my buddies are with me twenty-four seven anyway. When I did look at names, I took a picture of Larry Robinson's name and Bob Gainey's name. I also searched out other Canadiens greats like Yvan Cournoyer, Steve Shutt, and all those guys. When I broke into the NHL, a lot of ex–Canadiens players had bars in downtown Montreal. On a weekly basis, the players would go over and hang out and have a couple drinks at a bar owned by a former Canadiens great. When I looked at names on the Cup, I ended up only looking at players from the Canadiens.

"I was never a hockey fan growing up. When I was kid, I didn't have posters and jerseys of hockey players on my bedroom walls. I never grew up dreaming that I would play hockey in the NHL. When I was growing up in Wisconsin, all the other kids were fans of players on the Chicago Blackhawks. The only guy that I had a jersey of growing up was Bill White because I always wore number two when I played, and Bill wore number two. I didn't watch them play that often on TV, because I wasn't a big hockey fan. I would prefer to be outside playing sports instead of sitting in front of the TV, watching a game.

"I went to North Dakota originally to play football. I ended up playing football and hockey when I was there. I had a few trophies; that is about it. So, when I had the Cup, I didn't stare at all these names. I was more interested in the Montreal Canadiens players. When you are playing for the Montreal Canadiens, it is as if you are playing for the Dallas Cowboys or the New York Yankees. There is a history there and you can go back decades with the Canadiens. When you are playing for them, you are dialed in to the history of the team. As a player, you would meet some of those guys at events. These guys are legends, and I was in the world of Montreal hockey. I didn't know a lot about that world as a kid or when I was coming out of college. I never expected to play a game in Montreal when I showed up. I was convinced that I was going to Nova Scotia to play in the AHL. Then I made the team and the next thing I knew, all these legends I started to hear about, they were right there at all the games."

Picking a favorite photo from the summer of 1999 is difficult for Ludwig.

"I have one photo of me with the Cup along with Dad and my grandpa. The other one I love was taken on that big houseboat. It was such a great time, and it was packed with all these great people. My best friend, who passed away a few years ago, was standing in the middle of the boat, and he is a big dude, and is wearing one of those classic orange life jackets. The life jacket barely fits him, and he is holding the Stanley Cup up in the air. That photo was taken by a friend of mine, we called her Kato. Kato took the photo with one of those portable throwaway cameras. I blew up that photo to about ten feet long by three feet high. I used to hang it in my game room in Wisconsin. The photo is kind of grainy, but that is the picture that is probably my favorite from my time with the Cup. The people in that photo were the closest to me and some of them are not here anymore. That is why I love the photo so much. I'm able to see them, remember them, and think back to the good times we had with the Stanley Cup."

To someone like Craig Ludwig, life doesn't get much better than that.

And none of it would have been possible had Ludwig decided to retire after the previous season. Instead, he helped the 1999 Dallas Stars etch their names into hockey history. Ludwig also had his own "John Elway" moment and went out like a champion. Even better, little Eagle River, Wisconsin, had an experience they will never forget.

CHAPTER 6

Larry Robinson, a True Legend

2000 New Jersey Devils
Larry Robinson

The word *legend* is thrown around far too often in sports, but what other term could you use when describing Larry Robinson?

He won six Stanley Cups as a player, three as an assistant coach, and one as a head coach. Beginning in the 1970s, he won a Stanley Cup in five different decades.

This humble kid who grew up on a dairy farm in rural Ontario won more Stanley Cups than some of the biggest icons in the history of the NHL. Consider that Gordie Howe won the Stanley Cup four times in his career; same with Wayne Gretzky.

Few people know more about the joy of being a Stanley Cup champion than the Hall of Fame defenseman who was a key member of the Canadiens' fabled "big three" in the 1970s.

Robinson first won the Stanley Cup with the Canadiens as a young player in 1973. Three years later, he played a vital role in the Montreal Canadiens' remarkable run of four straight Stanley Cups. That

Canadiens team is still considered one of the greatest dynasties in the history of the NHL. In the 1976 and 1977 Stanley Cup playoffs, the Canadiens had a 24–3 record. Robinson was one of nine Hall of Famers on this remarkable team.

In the 1976–77 season, the Canadiens only lost eight games in the regular season, and then only two in their run to another Stanley Cup. For a lot of people, me included, the 1976–77 Canadiens are the greatest NHL team ever assembled. Robinson won the Norris Trophy as the NHL's best defenseman that year. The next season, Robinson, or "Big Bird" as he was known to his teammates, won the coveted Conn Smythe Trophy as the MVP of the playoffs. Robinson won the Stanley Cup again with the Canadiens in 1986.

He won a Cup as an assistant coach with the Devils in 1995. He won a Cup as the head coach of the Devils in 2000. He won another Cup as the assistant coach (again) of the Devils in 2003. And then he won another Cup with the St. Louis Blues in 2019 as their senior consultant of hockey operations.

That is ten Stanley Cup rings over five decades, one for every finger.

Officially, players started to get a day with the Cup in the 1990s. However, thanks to the power of that Montreal Canadiens dynasty, there

Larry Robinson and his wife on the far left, along with friends from Kentucky

were exceptions. While the Cup didn't tour the world, it took an impromptu trip throughout Quebec that few people knew about at the time. Robinson remembers vividly how Guy Lafleur, the Canadiens' biggest star at the time, decided to take matters into his own hands.

"Guy Lafleur took the Cup out of the back of Claude Mouton's car back home to Thurso, Quebec, to take pictures with it. A few things like that happened and the Cup got damaged a bit, so years later, they decided to have someone take care of it."

Hockey historian and author Liam Maguire says Lafleur's Stanley Cup escapade is worthy of a movie.

"Guy was best friends with someone by the name of Pierre Plouffe. Pierre is still alive, and he lives in Mont-Tremblant. Pierre is one of the wildest characters you will ever meet in your life. Pierre won the Canadian master's water-skiing championship numerous times," says Maguire.

"The guy who had the Cup that day for the Montreal Canadiens was their public relations director, a gentleman by the name of Claude Mouton. He was also the longtime public address announcer in the Montreal Forum for years and had a very distinct voice. In 1978, Guy Lafleur took the Cup out of the back of Claude Mouton's car. Claude had the Cup and Guy told him, 'I just need to borrow it for an hour.' Guy and Pierre didn't just take the Cup to Thurso for a few hours. That Cup was gone for almost two full days! Claude Mouton was freaking out, thinking the Cup was long gone. Guy called him up and said, 'Don't worry, we got it. We will bring it back tomorrow. Just relax.'

"Back then, you just were not supposed to do that with the Cup. But it was Guy Lafleur in 1978—the rules did not apply to him. Years later, Pierre told me that he dared Guy to do it, and Lafleur said, 'Sure, I am in.' And they took it!"

Unlike Lafleur, Robinson never got his chance to spend a day with the Cup in those years.

Robinson grew up in a small town in eastern Ontario, not too far from the Quebec border, and to him, sharing the Cup was especially important. Finally, in 1995, when he won the Cup as an assistant coach with the Devils, it was Robinson's turn to spend a day with the trophy that he had won so many times.

"I got to take the Cup home a couple of times. In 1995, I took the Cup back to the farm where I grew up in Marvelville, Ontario. From there I took the Cup to my brother-in-law's restaurant that night. The first time I had the Cup, it was like a dream. All of a sudden, I had the Stanley Cup to myself for a day. I went to my hometown, and I would see all these people and their reaction to the Cup. I saw people in their seventies and eighties who had never seen the Stanley Cup before. They had grown up watching it on TV, and all of a sudden, they could touch the Cup and take a picture with it. A lot of them had tears coming down their faces. That is when it hit me: *Holy mackerel, being that close to the Cup can be a very emotional thing.*"

Robinson is proud of the tiny community.

"Growing up, I went to a one-room school in Marvelville, out in the middle of nowhere in eastern Ontario. I was there from grade one through grade eight at this one-room school. When I left grade eight and went to high school, the one-room school closed and became a community center. The second time that I had the Cup [in 2000], I took it to my high school, and we had a big celebration there.

"The next time I had the Cup, in 2003, I took it down to where I live in Plant City, Florida. Plant City is the strawberry capital of Florida. We get a lot of people from Michigan and Chicago that come to stay there. I took the Cup to the local bar, Beef 'O' Brady's. I knew the owner. When I got there in the afternoon, there was this big lineup all the way around the side of this shopping center where the bar is located. I looked, and they were almost all Red Wings fans! The Red Wings fans there ended up joining us and got to spend a day with the Cup.

"The last time I had the Cup, in 2019 with St. Louis, I took the

Cup back to where I used to live in Bradenton, Florida. I took it to a police station, the fire department, and then to visit another Beef 'O' Brady's. From there I took it to the development where I live and all the people in the development could come in and spend time with the Cup and take pictures."

Robinson considers himself a lucky man to have his name engraved on the Cup so many times, and even luckier to have shared the thrill of victory with his family.

"I was fortunate. My daughter and her husband and their twin boys, they came and spent time with us in St. Louis when we won the Cup. They came in the parade with me on the same truck; that was frigging awesome. The kids got to throw the beads into the crowd. That was one of the best experiences that I had with the Cup."

When you have won the Stanley Cup as many times as Robinson, choosing a favorite would be hard. However, there is one that stands out among the rest.

"Winning the Cup in 2000 was special for me, because that was my first head coaching job. I took over as the head coach with eight games left in the regular season. Lou [Lamoriello] brought me in to replace Robbie Ftorek.

"We were a really good team, but it was a team that didn't know how good they could be. Our team changed when Alexander Mogilny joined the Devils. Even in practices, I could see everything keep getting better and the intensity went higher.

"The players and I went through a lot together that Cup run. The longer we lasted in the playoffs, the more we became a team. The more we became a team, the more we became a family. Even now, when we have a reunion of the 2000 Devils team, the camaraderie that you see with that group was kind of like what we had in Montreal during the seventies when we won four in a row. Guys that would play for each other and wanted to do well for each other."

That Cup win stands out as a unique experience.

"Coaches today have a lot of resources to work with. In 2000, we didn't have anyone like a spotter or anything like that. We had a VHS machine and some tape that we would play forward and backward. We would have to remember the time-stamp number on the VHS player so you could remember which part of the play you wanted to show the team. For those who have never used a VHS before, there was a time stamp on the tape that would show up in the corner of the TV screen. This allowed you to forward or rewind to the exact spot you were looking for.

"During the Conference Finals against the Flyers, after we lost game four and we were down three to one in the series, I stayed up until two thirty in the morning, watching videotape. At two thirty in the morning, I recognized something that I saw. I don't know why, it just hit me as I watched the tape. I realized something the Flyers were doing—it was being done the same way all the time. I made my coaching adjustments based on that and wrote them all down that night.

"The next morning at the team meeting, I told the players and made that adjustment. Sure enough, it worked to a T. I couldn't have drawn that up any better.

"Watching video, I noticed that every time that the Flyers dumped the puck into our end, they sent one guy deep on the forecheck and two guys along the boards, opposite of the puck. They did it every single time they dumped the puck in. At the team meeting I told Marty [Martin Brodeur] to not play the puck, no matter what. He was to stay in the net, and I wanted our defenseman to play the puck. Our defenseman would take the hit, get the puck to our center, and we had an instant breakout play. Nine times out of ten we ended up with a two-on-one or a three-on-two. We were constantly catching three of their players deep in our end on one play. You don't mind getting next to no sleep for over two months when you have coaching moments like that.

"I thought the Flyers might make an adjustment of their own afterwards, but they never did. As a result, it worked in our favor, and we ended up winning the series in seven games and moved on to the Cup Final."

It was a tough series, with the deciding game six going to double overtime. But Jason Arnott scored, and the Devils beat the Stars to become Stanley Cup champions. Robinson admits his Cup celebrations in the summer of 2000 were more subdued than in previous years.

"I was so spent mentally and physically after winning the Cup in 2000, it was kind of a blessing just to have the Cup. I could sit back and watch everyone else celebrate. I didn't have anything left in the tank at that point, I was totally drained."

That was also the summer that Robinson changed his drink of choice out of the Stanley Cup.

"I am not a big champagne drinker, but I did take a sip of champagne out of the Cup. Most of the time, I drank beer from the Cup."

As much he loves to party, Robinson did have a limit on what he would allow to be consumed out of the Cup.

"The only time I got upset by what someone put in the Cup was when I brought the Cup back to my hometown. After I won the Cup as an assistant coach with the Devils in 1995, I took the Cup back home to Marvelville, Ontario. One of my relatives came over and brought a Jersey cow. He thought it would be funny to have a Jersey cow eating out of the Stanley Cup. Well, when they put the feed into the Cup, I was not a happy camper."

As someone who has their name etched into the Stanley Cup so many times, Robinson understands the magical powers of the trophy.

"You have to remember, the Stanley Cup is extremely popular. Wherever it went, people just went nuts over the Cup. That's when they created the Keepers of the Cup and made the idea of sharing the Cup an ongoing thing."

For a man who has raised the Stanley Cup over his head a remarkable ten times, Robinson says it has nothing to do with him. It is all about the teams that he has been a part of.

"I played with a lot of great players. Hockey is a big team sport, we used to say in Montreal; individuals win awards, but a *team* wins a championship. The reason we were so successful in Montreal, we were always a team. It didn't matter if you were Guy Lafleur, or [Maurice] 'Rocket' Richard, you were all treated the same way.

"I was very blessed that I got to play in a great organization in Montreal. We were taught the meaning of hard work and sacrifice and dedication and discipline. That cornerstone set me up for my future career."

Robinson feels privileged to be a part of the famed Canadiens dynasty.

"Out of all the Cups that I won, the team that I feel the closest to is the seventies Canadiens team when we won four in a row. That was a group that stayed together for a long time. You can have the best team in the world; it doesn't always mean you will win. From those Montreal teams, we are still close. From Guy Lapointe to Steve Shutt to Jacques Lemaire, I still converse with them a lot. We are still really close.

"You need a little bit of luck on your side too, and we had that as well. More importantly, we had a great team in Montreal. I was happy to be a part of something special and do whatever was asked of me to win."

It's hard to argue with a ten-time Cup-winning champion, but it seems having Larry Robinson on your side helps even more.

CHAPTER 7

The Unlikely Champions

2001 Colorado Avalanche
Dan Hinote and Eric Messier

When folk singer John Denver released the hit song "Rocky Mountain High" in 1972, little did he know that it would be a perfect soundtrack to the Stanley Cup run of the 2001 Colorado Avalanche. This was the year that Ray Bourque, one of the great players in the NHL for the previous two decades, finally won that all-elusive Stanley Cup.

Not only that, but the Avs won on home ice, in Colorado.

In one of the most iconic memories of the NHL playoffs, immediately after receiving the Stanley Cup from commissioner Gary Bettman, captain Joe Sakic handed it to a teary-eyed Bourque.

The 2001 Avalanche featured stars like Sakic, Bourque, and Patrick Roy, but it also featured a number of depth players who ended up playing a key role for the team in the run to the Cup.

Work Hard, Play Hard

Dan Hinote might have one of the most unusual paths to the Stanley Cup that most people have heard of.

Hinote was born in Florida, but he was raised in Minnesota. From there Dan spent two years at the US Military Academy at West Point, America's exclusive military college, the school that produced such iconic generals as George S. Patton and Norman Schwarzkopf Jr. After two years going to school and playing hockey at West Point, Hinote went from one extreme to another, and started playing for the OHL's Oshawa Generals.

Hinote said the way he was raised helped him adjust to life at West Point. "Going from regular life to West Point was a transition on its own. But my dad is old-school, so I was brought up with that kind

of daily discipline. But at West Point, there was a lot more structure and we had to have our beds made perfectly and we did a lot of shoe-shining to meet the standards," says Hinote.

"I attended West Point for financial reasons. Our family didn't have a lot of money and at the same time I wanted to become an FBI agent. We were able to let West Point know that I wanted to play hockey there. I still had to meet their academic entrance requirements before they accepted. But once they said yes, my family knew that I would be able to play hockey and get a good education for free.

"I ended up becoming the first hockey player from West Point drafted into the NHL at the end of his second year. West Point has a loophole, if you leave before the start of your third year, you don't have to serve four years in the army. My parents said that since I was drafted by the Avalanche, I should give my best shot at playing in the NHL. The head scout of the Avs, Dave Draper, had a connection with the Oshawa Generals and got me signed there. I knew the Generals were a good team and I couldn't wait to get there. True story, prior to showing up to Generals training camp, I had never been to Canada."

Needless to say, Hinote faced a jarring transition from prim and proper West Point to riding the bus with the Oshawa Generals in the OHL.

"Going from West Point to the Oshawa Generals turned out to be a bigger challenge. To go from a rigid lifestyle at West Point and then to major junior hockey in the OHL, that was a big transition. In the OHL, we were pretty much on our own during the day. It took some getting used to," says Hinote.

After paying his dues in the OHL, Hinote became a full-time player for the Avalanche at the start of the 2000–01 season. Going into training camp, the Avs were already thinking about a deep playoff run.

"The expectations were high that year. We knew that it was probably going to be Ray's last year. We also had made the Rob Blake trade in

February. The whole time that 2001 team was together, they expected to win the whole thing. At the end of the year, if we didn't win the Cup, we would have been surprised," says Hinote.

"It wasn't spoken; there was a sense of urgency with Ray. We all wanted to win the Cup for ourselves obviously; but helping Ray win was a special thing too."

During the postseason, fate intervened and Hinote ended up playing a more important role in their Cup run. Peter Forsberg got hurt and coach Bob Hartley put Hinote on a line with two superstars.

"Bob Hartley was playing some gamesmanship with the lines, and he put me with Alex Tanguay and Joe Sakic to start game seven of the Cup Final," says Hinote. "It was an unbelievable experience, and I was fortunate enough to play with such great players. They make it all look easy."

It was an emotional moment for Raymond Bourque, and it was an emotional moment for Hinote and the rest of the Avs.

"Because Ray is such a good human being, it is hard to explain how much it meant to us. We all teared up watching Joe hand Ray the Cup. For a young hockey player, that isn't a typical reaction. The whole thing was very emotional; we felt a part of his journey to climbing that mountain. We did it for ourselves, and we knew that we would go down in history as part of *that* Cup team," said Hinote.

To this day, Hinote still gets chills when he sees images of Bourque raising the Cup.

"Every time the Stanley Cup playoffs come on the TV, they show Ray raising the Cup. It brings me back to that night every time that I see it."

After Bourque had his turn with the Cup, Hinote couldn't wait for his. It was a night for Hinote to share his Cup glory with a group of people who made everything possible.

"The cool thing about hockey is that there are so many people responsible for your success. From your peewee coach to your captain in college, you name it, somebody has had an effect at every level of your hockey career. That is what I was thinking about as I raised the Cup over my head. I knew where my family and friends were sitting in the stands, so I made sure to be facing them. To me it was our Cup, not just my Cup. They were all the people that helped me get there."

After the parades and celebrations, Hinote couldn't wait to bring the Cup to his hometown of Elk River, Minnesota.

"It was great when I got a chance to raise the Cup that night. I had a lot of family there and some friends. My captain from West Point was there as well, Ian Winer," says Hinote.

"Joel Otto was from Elk River. He had won the Cup when he was with Calgary in 1989. When he won, he brought the Cup to his cabin in rural Minnesota. Once I won the Cup, the city of Elk River was excited about the possibility of the Cup coming to town. Joel took it to the cabin, so Elk River hadn't seen the Cup yet. I remember thinking as a kid if I ever won the Cup, I would bring it to Elk River and take it to the rink," said Hinote. "Then I won it, and everybody in town was going crazy, they were so excited about the Cup. Once I won, all the questions came out. 'What are you going to do with the Cup?' I wanted to bring it to the rink, share it with the city, and make sure that everybody had access to it. I also took it to the local bar so people could drink out of it. It was a great experience and a great way to give back to the community that did so much for me."

Hinote got the Cup in late July 2001. "It was a typical Minnesota summer day, eighty-five degrees and humid with tons of mosquitoes."

Hinote says he didn't do anything out of the ordinary with the Cup, aside from "eating and drinking almost everything out of the Cup when we had it."

However, he did have more time with the Cup than he was expecting.

"What happened was that I got the Cup a day early. I received a call from a random number, and it was Mike Bolt from the Hockey Hall of Fame, one of the Keepers of the Cup. He said, 'Hey, your trainer is finished with the Cup.' Well, he was in St. Cloud, and that is only an hour away. He said, 'You can have the Cup tonight if you want it.' Everybody was already in town, hanging out at the house, preparing for the Cup's arrival the next morning. I immediately said, 'Of course I want it tonight!'

"I asked Mike, 'Can you meet me at the Dairy Queen in Elk River?' I asked a bunch of my friends if they wanted to go to DQ. I had to talk them into it, but they finally said yes. When we pulled into the Dairy Queen, Mike Bolt's limo was waiting there. Mike was standing outside of the limo with his white gloves on and the Cup in his hands. When they saw that, all my friends went crazy.

"I called this bar in Minneapolis called Williams. I asked the manager, 'I have the Cup, would you guys mind setting up a little area for us?' Even though this was a last-second request, they rolled out the red carpet for us when we arrived with the Cup. It was a ton of fun and me and all my friends had a great time. It turned into quite a wild evening. Now, I wasn't supposed to get the Cup until the following morning, and we had a tent set up outside my parents' house in anticipation of the arrival of the Cup. My mom had friends from work coming over early so they could take a picture with the Cup before they went to work. Needless to say, it was a late night for me and my friends.

"The next morning my mom came into my room and woke me up and she was a little perturbed. She said, 'Can you get those *bodies* out of the front yard?!' I was like, 'Yeah, sure, Mom.' I walked out to the front yard and there must have been eight of my friends sleeping in the yard and out in the tent we had set up. They had no blankets or anything; they were just sleeping. I looked at the scene and my mom's coworkers were about to show up at any minute.

"Since I got the Cup early, we must have eaten seven meals out of the Cup and lots of drinks. I also had the experience of walking around the streets of Minneapolis with the Cup.

"Minnesota might as well be Canada when it comes to the hallowed ground that the Cup is on. That was pretty cool, to see random people react to the Cup and hang out with the Cup."

Hinote said it was fascinating to see how people reacted.

"Some people were in such awe of the Cup; they didn't want to touch it because they had too much respect for it and didn't earn it. There were some people who didn't play anymore and they wouldn't touch it. There were some young players who didn't want to touch it, because they felt they would play in the NHL one day. Guys like Nate Prosser and Paul Martin, who both went on to the NHL, are from the Elk River area and they wouldn't touch it. I loved that.

"There was an older couple that was crying when they got near the Cup. They thought they would never see it up close. The power of the Cup is such an unexplainable thing. For something that is just a trophy, to have such a big effect on everybody is something to see."

Like all other players, when Hinote finally had a quiet moment, he started searching out names on the Cup.

"I went through almost all the names on the Cup. You have to! You don't know if you are ever going to have this chance again. Growing up in Minnesota, the Stanley Cup wasn't a thing with the North Stars, then the team left for Dallas. I love the history of the Cup. A name that meant a lot to me was Bryan Trottier. He was our assistant coach with the Avs that year and I looked up all the Cups that he won. I have a photo of me, Bryan, and the Cup. Bryan had a big effect on my career, and also he is such an amazing human being. And to top it off, he was a great player. And his name is all over that trophy!"

Looking back, Hinote is still amazed that his name is on the Stanley Cup.

"To me, I was just a hockey player. It is all surprising to me when someone wants my autograph. Or someone tells you that they looked up to you."

Hockey is a humble sport that way.

"It is a cool thing knowing my name is on the Cup and it will be on the trophy in the Hall of Fame for a while. I have a son and a daughter who have seen the Cup and they have seen my name on it. They are young and don't quite grasp the significance of it, but they know it's cool. What is nice is by the time they do understand it, the Cup and my name will still be around."

Hinote has little trouble picking out his favorite photo during his time with the Cup.

"I have a big group picture of everyone that showed up in Elk River for my day with the Cup. It makes me laugh out loud every time that I see it. It is instant happiness when I see that photo. I see it, and my heart rate jumps, and my energy goes up."

Les Boys

Eric Messier's path to the Stanley Cup was even more indirect than Hinote's. In fact, there are few players who could say they went through what Messier had to in order to be a Stanley Cup champion.

Seven years before he won a Stanley Cup with the Avalanche, Eric Messier was playing beer league hockey and working towards his university degree. A victim of the 1994 lockout, Messier didn't have a lot of options.

"When I was twenty-one years old, it was 1994 and there was a lockout," says Messier. "No team had a training camp. I was done playing junior hockey and I didn't have a chance to go to any NHL training camps or even an AHL training camp. I ended up playing in

a beer league back home in Drummondville, Quebec. I was going to university, but I was only allowed to attend school after Christmas, because I didn't finish all of my CEGEP credits. After that, I went to the University of Quebec. Until then, I played weekend beer league hockey with my buddies."

Playing beer league with his buddies and going to school seemed like Messier's future, until Bob Hartley came into his life.

"I played against Bob Hartley three years when I played in the QMJHL. He coached in Laval. My first year in junior, I was in Trois-Rivières, then the team moved to Sherbrooke." Bob recruited Messier to play for him with the AHL's Cornwall Aces, which was then the farm team for the Colorado Avalanche.

At the start of the 1996–97 season, Bob Hartley took over as the head coach of the Hershey Bears, now the top farm team for the Colorado Avalanche. Hartley and Messier went on to win the Calder Cup as AHL champions together in 1997. Four years later, Hartley and Messier teamed up to win the Stanley Cup, a fact that Messier is very proud of.

"I was the only player to win both Cups with him," says Eric. "Bob knew how to talk to his players to get the best out of them. He knew me and knew exactly how to motivate me. I knew what my job was in Colorado. I was not there to score goals, my job was to block shots, to finish my checks. I was a grinder who played on the third and the fourth line. My job was to not allow the other team any chance to score, especially their best players. I also played on the penalty kill, so I knew the reason I was there and what was expected of me."

Messier ended up being a part of an effective line that also featured Stéphane Yelle and Shjon Podein.

"We had a chance to play together for three years, and that 2000–2001 season was by far my best year in the NHL. Stéphane had the experience of winning the Cup with the Avs in 1996. Shjon lost in the Cup Final with the Flyers in 1997. Those two guys had a lot of experience in the playoffs, and I was lucky to play with them. In game five of the Cup Final, I was robbed of a rare goal by a great save from Martin Brodeur. After all these years, I still remember that save and how close I came to scoring in the Stanley Cup Final."

For a role player, Messier ended up getting a lot of ice time in game six and game seven.

"The good thing about my role with the Avs, when we got up by one or two goals, I was playing more. I was more of a defensive guy, and they used me a lot in those roles. At times I would take a face-off in the defensive zone; when the puck was cleared from our zone, I would go for a change."

Once the Avs won it all, Messier patiently waited for his turn to skate around with the Cup.

"Alex Tanguay gave me the Cup, then after I skated around, I gave it to Chris Dingman. I was about the tenth or eleventh guy on the team that got the Cup after we won. All the veterans, Joe Sakic, Patrick Roy, all had the Cup first," says Messier. "I was lucky. All of my family was there that night and also one of my best friends. Over twenty years later, I still remember that night like it was yesterday."

After the celebrations died down, it was time to organize the Cup's summer tour.

"I got the call at the end of June letting me know when I would get the Cup. I was scheduled to get married on Saturday, July seventh. They asked me if I wanted the Stanley Cup for my wedding. I said, 'No, I want the Cup to party with. The wedding is not the best place for that kind of party.' I ended up getting the Cup on Tuesday, July third. It was a big week for me. I had the Cup in the middle of the week, then I got married that Saturday. I didn't get much sleep that week.

"I first had the Cup in Sorel, Quebec, in the morning," continues Messier. "Afterwards, I took the Cup to my hometown in Drummond-ville, Quebec. In the afternoon I took the Cup to my parents' house in Saint-Germain, which is about five minutes outside of Drummondville. From there I took the Cup to a local sports bar. When I played beer league with my buddies during the 1994 lockout, we would all hang out at this other bar after our games were over. I took the Cup there until at least two in the morning. Some of my friends and neighbors from Colorado were coming to town for my upcoming wedding. They ended up showing up at the last bar as I celebrated with my friends.

"That night with the Cup at the last bar was like the well-known Quebec movie *Les Boys*," adds Messier, citing the cult film about an amateur hockey team. "It was almost the same thing. The guys were younger, and the owner of the bar was our coach sometimes. It really was like a scene from the movie. We had beer and champagne out of the Cup and had a good time. Now, we were not supposed to do this. And this was before cell phones, so nobody else could take a picture. But I had my puppy, Oscar, eating his food out of the Cup the next morning. Hey, he was part of the family too!

"My parents met me at my house in Sorel when the Cup arrived. As soon as I got the Cup, I right away gave it to my dad. That was the first time in my life I saw my dad cry, while he was standing there, holding the Stanley Cup. He was so happy. After we left my friend's bar, we got back home around three in the morning. We ordered pizza and me and my buddies started reading names off the Cup. We looked at almost all of the names. Seeing the names of players like Jean Béliveau and Maurice Richard, they are legends, and now I am going to have my name on the Cup with them. That was a special feeling. I never saw Maurice Richard play, but I met him when I was playing junior. I was so speechless when I met him, I didn't even say a word. In Quebec, Maurice Richard was the biggest name in hockey.

"We were eating pizza and reading off names, 'Wayne Gretzky! Guy Lafleur!'

"These are all the big names of hockey," continues Messier, "and all their names are on the Cup. I could not believe that my name was going to be with them on that trophy. Around five in the morning, the pizza was gone, and we had read almost all the names on there. A few hours later, one of our neighbors showed up to get a picture with the Cup. He was in his late sixties or early seventies. When he picked up the Cup, he was crying, because he had a chance to see Maurice Richard play when he was younger. To see the Cup in person and to see Richard's name on it was overwhelming to him.

"On July fourth at noon, the Hockey Hall of Fame took the Cup back. I was up all day and all night that I had the Cup. I didn't get much sleep the next day, because all of my friends from Colorado were in town. We went golfing and then went out to dinner in Montreal. The Friday before my wedding I got a little bit of rest, but not much. Both my wife and I could barely talk on our wedding day; we both lost our voice in the days leading up to the big day. Friday night, before she went to sleep, my wife had Vicks on her throat, the old grandma remedy. It worked, though. She got her voice back on Saturday; it was a miracle.

"I went to the Hockey Hall of Fame in Toronto with my son in 2011 and we saw the Cup and he saw my name on the Cup. He was with his school on a class trip at the Hall of Fame. My son was the only one allowed to touch the Cup, because his dad had won it! To see him with the Cup, looking at my name, that was a great moment.

"The Stanley Cup is the toughest trophy to win in all of sports and it is the only one to have all the names on it."

Eric Messier, a guy who used to play beer league hockey, has his name etched on the same trophy as Maurice Richard, Wayne Gretzky, and Guy Lafleur.

CHAPTER 8

Shanny's Big Adventure

2002 Detroit Red Wings
Brendan Shanahan

Growing up in the west-end Toronto neighborhood of Mimico, Brendan Shanahan was one of four brothers who loved playing sports. While his older brother Brian became a star lacrosse player, Brendan would go on to become one of the top-scoring NHL forwards of his generation.

By the time he started playing organized hockey and lacrosse when he was four years old, Brendan's older brothers, Danny, Brian, and Shaun, were already fifteen, twelve, and ten, respectively. Even though he was the little kid in the family compared to the rest of them, his older brothers always let him play ball hockey. Brendan quickly dominated hockey and lacrosse in his age group and began to play an age group up by the time he was six years old. With a lot of support from his brothers and the rest of his family, Brendan scored many goals in hockey and lacrosse. One time, he scored nine goals in a lacrosse game against the best competition in his age group. While his older brothers played B-level hockey, Brendan emerged as one of the best players on one of the best AAA teams in the province. To his brothers' amazement, even from a young age, excelling at hockey and lacrosse came so easy for him.

Shanahan ended up scoring 656 goals during his career and he was a big part of a Detroit Red Wings team that won three Stanley Cups in 1997, 1998, and 2002. What some people tend to forget is that Shanahan played ten years in the NHL before he was able to lift the Stanley Cup over his head.

"I started my career in New Jersey and then I left as a free agent for St. Louis. I felt like I was part of good teams that had the ability to at least challenge for the Stanley Cup. The one year I had in Hartford, it was really a rebuilding team in a city where they were looking to move the franchise. Suddenly I felt further away from the Stanley Cup than ever before."

Shanahan's fortunes changed dramatically on October 9, 1996, when he landed in Detroit after a multiplayer deal that involved Paul Coffey heading to the Whalers.

"I was excited about joining a team that had the potential to break a forty-year drought since they last won the Cup. But the year before we'd also missed the playoffs in Hartford. And so, for me, coming to Detroit, there was an appreciation. It was an education too, that it is a privilege to be on a team that is capable of competing for the Stanley Cup."

Shanahan knew right away that he was a part of something special when he joined the Red Wings.

"I had joined a great team. They had a lot of centermen. When I was first traded to Detroit, I looked at the roster. Someone had asked who I was going to play with. I said, 'It really doesn't matter.' Their centers were Yzerman, Fedorov, Larionov, and Draper. I didn't think they were putting me on the checking line. So, it didn't matter what line they put me on; our three top centers were all great.

The Wings also had Scotty Bowman as coach, whom Shanahan had the utmost respect for.

"With Scotty, you just knew there was one man in charge. Scotty was not a warm and cuddly communicating kind of person with us. We were a veteran team, and we didn't need hugs from our coach. What we wanted were wins. Scotty knew how to push buttons and he kept a distance from the players. I always say this: During games, a player faces the ice, and their back is to the coach. A player's focus is on the game. However, a player can hear that voice behind them, and they know when that person is lost, and they know when that person is pushing all the right buttons and making all the right decisions. Sitting on the bench, the Red Wings players felt that with Scotty back there, we were fine. When we were in big moments and we were in big games, we knew our coach was better than the other team's coach. We just knew that Scotty was not going to be outcoached."

Sure enough, in spring 1997, the Red Wings went on a deep playoff run. For the Cup Final they faced Eric Lindros and the Philadelphia Flyers, a big, punishing team with their Legion of Doom. Four games later, Brendan Shanahan was finally a Stanley Cup champion.

Like so many players, Shanahan had dreamed about this moment all his life. But he was surprised by what he felt when it finally came.

"The biggest emotion I felt was relief. This was my tenth season in the NHL and I was in the middle of my career. I felt a lot of things. I had gratitude, I was elated, but the biggest thing was relief. I could breathe because I had just done something that is really hard to do."

Shanahan still smiles at a scene that unfolded in the dying seconds of their clinching game.

"There is a great moment in the final game with six seconds left to play and there is a face-off in the neutral zone. We were up three to nothing in the series and we had a two-one lead. You would think that the neutral zone face-off with six seconds to go is the time to start to envision what the Stanley Cup celebration is going to be like. Steve Yzerman was taking the draw and Darren McCarty and I were both lined up on the right wing to protect any play through the middle.

"Fast-forward to after we won, and we were watching this video of the season recap. I looked at our faces and we were all crazy intense, our eyes looked like we were on fire, and we were yelling instructions to each other. I watched the video and at first, I couldn't figure out when it took place because I rarely played with McCarty, and we were both lined up on the same side. In the video it was a tight shot, and you could only see our faces. Then it hit me, *Oh my god*, that is the face-off with six seconds to go in the Cup Final. I liked that moment because with six seconds left to play, we were not thinking about the Stanley Cup, we were thinking about doing our job. That, to me, is a reminder of the kind of focus our entire team had that 1997 playoff run."

After a quick visit to *The Tonight Show with Jay Leno*, Shanahan was excited to get his day with the Stanley Cup.

"I got the Cup at the time of my oldest brother's birthday and it worked out in such a way that I got two days with the Cup, not just one. The first night the plan was, let's all pile in a bus and go barhopping. We took the Cup all over Mimico and downtown Toronto. The

Cup arrived in the evening on a Friday, and we were ready to go! We took the Cup to the Blue Goose in Mimico and a few other local bars."

More than just a player, Shanahan is a true hockey fan, and he loves the history of the game. That is why he was excited to look at names on the Cup when he had some quiet time.

"Growing up, in your imagination, when you are in your driveway or playing road hockey, the 'next goal wins' is always for the Stanley Cup. It was a wonderful thing when I had the Cup, to look at some of the names on the trophy. I had heard stories and I looked up mis-spellings and the name of a dog that had been crossed off it. I wanted to see the stuff I heard about and read about. Then you see names like Bobby Clarke, Phil Esposito, Ken Dryden, Gordie Howe, Ted Lindsay, and Dave Keon. These were all players I idolized and to see their names on the Cup was amazing."

Shanahan's second day with the Cup led to an unscheduled, yet special, personal moment.

"The next day was more subdued. We had a big picnic at my mom's house for the neighborhood kids and the plan was to hold another event later that evening. I had the Cup at Mom's house and there was a bit of a gap between the gathering at her place, and then the event at the Left Bank," a popular nightclub in downtown Toronto at the time. "That is when I snuck the Stanley Cup to the cemetery that my father is buried at. I was by myself, and it was a beautiful, sunny summer day. I was nervous about bringing the Cup to a place like that because I didn't want to be disrespectful to other people. It just so happened that when I arrived it was completely empty. Even then, I wasn't sure if I would bring the Cup out of the car. But I did, and I sat where my father is laid to rest. I spent time reflecting there. I quietly put the Cup back in my car without anybody noticing.

"I started driving home and I was feeling a little hungry. I thought, *I am going to stop by Apache Burgers in Etobicoke and bring the Cup there.* It wasn't planned, I just wanted an Apache burger and some half-and-half, the combo of fries and onion rings. Then we all got ready, and we had a big celebration at the Left Bank in downtown Toronto. And then the Cup was gone! I said goodbye to the Cup in the parking lot that night, and the Keeper of the Cup was off to see another player."

One year later, the Red Wings were Stanley Cup champions again, and this time also swept their opponent, the Washington Capitals, in four games. Shanahan said it felt different than the first time and made sure to mention a hilarious moment with their captain, Steve Yzerman.

"We won our second Cup in 1998 on the road. Prior to game four, the team had flown our family members and significant others into Washington. We had two planes of people, and we were all flying back to Detroit. After a short celebration in the dressing room, we were now at the airport. I get on the plane, and I am in an aisle seat near the back of the plane. Next to me is my then fiancée. Steve Yzerman was sitting next to me in the other aisle seat, next to his wife. Someone came onto the plane with the Cup and brought it to the back where we were sitting and plunked it down in the aisle right next to Steve and me.

"The adrenalin from the game was wearing off and Steve looked at the Cup with a big, satisfied smile on his face and said out loud, 'Oh fuck, another summer with you! I don't know if I can take it.' We howled.

"We all enjoyed our time with the Cup in 1998 and we still had our celebrations. I can't speak for anyone else; I just know that my celebrations in 1998 were a little more civilized than they were the year before. The first time winning the Stanley Cup is a feeling of euphoria and relief. All those same emotions are still there the second time, but the more dominant emotion was satisfaction. We all felt that put a historical stamp on our team because so few teams are able to win it more than once, let alone back-to-back.

"During any season, you have highs and lows. During that 1997–98 season, whenever we were in a low, we would hear, 'Once you have won, you are not as motivated as you were the first time.' Everyone on the team took real offense to that. Quite frankly, that had to be coming from someone who never won the Stanley Cup before. It is like an animal who had only been eating berries and shrubs its whole life, then it finally gets to eat meat. Once you win the Cup, it becomes even more painful every time you don't win after that. You expect to win every year.

"Early in my career I would think to myself, *Oh well, we didn't win this year. Gretzky won the Cup or Lemieux won the Cup.* Once you win, there's this feeling like this is something that I *have* to do every year. Even though you can't do that, the expectations change once you finally unlock the code and win your first Cup."

In the summer of 1998, Shanahan's Cup celebrations took place in a different hometown.

"The second year we won the Cup, I only had it for one day that summer. I was in Duxbury, Massachusetts, where my wife is from. I wanted a little bit of a quieter experience with the Cup that summer. We flew family and friends into Duxbury, which is outside of Boston. We had a fair-sized celebration in a party tent. But it was not the pub crawl that we had the year before."

By a twist of fate, Peter and Bobby Farrelly, Hollywood's Farrelly brothers, ended up being a part of the celebrations.

"My wife was picking something up at the local deli and Peter Farrelly, the Hollywood director, recognized her somehow. He introduced himself and said he and his brother were big hockey fans. Now, we had just moved to the area, but Peter said he and his brother would love to meet me at some point.

"My wife said, 'Well, we are having a Stanley Cup party this afternoon if you want to come by later.' And that's how I met Hollywood directors Peter and Bobby Farrelly. I also had some friends there from my time at Michael Power High School in Etobicoke. Longtime friends like Karen Stock and Phil Falcone were there."

During the 2001–02 season, Shanahan played eighty regular-season games and then another twenty-three in the playoffs. And that doesn't include six stress-filled games in the middle of the season for the Salt Lake City Winter Olympics, where he helped Team Canada beat the USA to win the Olympic gold medal. Now Shanahan and the rest of his veteran teammates had to prepare themselves for the grind of the playoffs.

"Our biggest challenge that year was keeping our composure. We went wire-to-wire that year in first place. We had a very good team, but in the NHL, very good teams don't always win. You run into a hot power play or a hot goalie, any team can lose in a seven-game series. We made a mistake by sitting some guys out in the last half-dozen games or so in the season. Scotty knew we had a lot of guys that were in their early to mid-thirties. A lot of us had been to the Olympics. In trying to rest us, we struggled in the last few games of the year.

"Then we lost our first two home games of the playoffs. I think a younger team might have panicked. But we locked it in game three and we won the next four games and eliminated Vancouver. Each series after that was difficult and we faced elimination in the third round and survived, then we won in five games in the Final against Carolina. Overall, with those three Cup-winning teams in Detroit, we were twelve and one in the Stanley Cup Final. That is a pretty good record."

After going through a drought at one point in the 2002 playoffs, Shanahan scored three goals in the final two games, including the game winner in the clinching game.

"I was a little snakebit prior to the Cup Final. In the playoffs, if you're snakebit, your season might be done, and you don't have time to sort it out and let the averages work themselves out. Then in the last two games I scored three goals, including two in the final. I'm glad the puck finally started going in at the proper time and I was able to help the team."

Shanahan's Stanley Cup celebrations that summer were much different than the first two. They included a stop on a small, quiet lake in Northern Ontario.

"My Stanley Cup day experiences are like the story of Goldilocks and the three bears. The first one was too hot! The second was in the middle. The third one was too cold! We didn't do much of anything that summer. I had a place up in Muskoka on a small lake in the area. We basically had the Stanley Cup sitting on the dock with us. We had no real parties planned and we just spent time with immediate family. The wildest thing we did that year was I knew that my high school friend Karen Stock was up at her cottage on Sugar Lake. I told her that I would swing by with the Stanley Cup and the Olympic gold medal. Karen did the rest as far as inviting some of our high school friends from back in Etobicoke. Hanging out with Karen on her dock, we got funny looks from people who were going by on their boats, and they would do a double take. You could almost hear them thinking, *Is that what we think it is?*

"After that, we went back home and went to dinner and brought the Cup into the restaurant with us. We were not going to leave it in the car by itself. It was a much quieter experience. I was thirty-three years old at the time and my wife was pregnant with twins. It was just as satisfying, though."

Family is especially important to Brendan Shanahan, and it was his family that led to his favorite photo from his three Stanley Cup wins.

"The first time I won the Stanley Cup in 1997, there is a photo of me on the ice lifting the Stanley Cup over my head. You can't tell by the photo where I am looking, but I know I am looking up at my family. At that moment, I found them in the crowd. It is a brief moment, but I remember it vividly, me seeing them and them seeing me with the Cup above my head for the first time. It looks like a typical photo of a guy on the ice with the Stanley Cup, but I know in this particular moment I looked up and found them, and our eyes were locked. That photo is very special to me."

As the current president of the Toronto Maple Leafs, Shanahan still hungers to be a part of another Stanley Cup celebration.

"What drives me now is more about wanting other people that I grew up with, and the city I grew up in, to experience what we got to in Detroit. That is what got me to accept the job in Toronto and that is what keeps me focused during any disappointment. It is what drives my determination when we have setbacks.

"It is all so that this city and this team that I grew up with can have that experience," Shanahan continues. "It is for people that I know but also just for the people of Toronto. Until I went to the NHL, I grew up with that same experience as other Leafs fans during the Harold Ballard years in Toronto.

"Winning is not at all about trying to get my name on the Cup again. It is so the people of Toronto can experience it."

To paraphrase an old saying, you can take the boy out of Mimico, but you can't take Mimico out of the boy.

CHAPTER 9

Sweden, Quebec, and Guy Lafleur

2004 Tampa Bay Lightning
Fredrik Modin and André Roy

Fredrik Modin and his brother Anders

With their back-to-back championships in 2020 and 2021 and a trip to the Cup Final in 2022, the Tampa Bay Lightning established themselves as the NHL's elite franchise during the pandemic era. That was definitely not always the case in their history. In fact, in the late 1990s, the Lightning were arguably the worst team in the NHL. For three straight years, the Lightning won fewer than twenty games in a season.

The only upside was some high draft picks. In 1998 they drafted both Vincent Lecavalier and Brad Richards. In 2000 they signed a free agent by the name of Martin St. Louis, a player later bound for the Hockey Hall of Fame.

Sleeping with the Cup

The year before they signed St. Louis, the Lighting acquired forward Fredrik Modin from the Toronto Maple Leafs. In Toronto, Modin was a favorite of both the fans and his teammates because of his powerful shot.

Growing up four hours north of Stockholm, Sweden, in Sundsvall, Modin played for the Njurunda Sports Club. If someone wanted to search for a picture showing what makes Sweden such a beautiful country, an aerial photo of Sundsvall would be all they need to see. Located on the northeast coast, Sundsvall has been named as one of the most beautiful cities in Sweden. Not far from the City of Stone, as Sundsvall is known in Sweden, you can find some of the most popular hiking trails and natural landscapes in the entire country.

In the 2003–04 season Modin scored twenty-nine goals and then added another eight goals and nineteen points in the postseason. In their game seven win over the Calgary Flames, Modin set up Ruslan Fedotenko's opening goal.

When the final seconds ticked off, Freddy Modin was a Stanley Cup champion. Two years later he became a member of the coveted Triple Gold Club, having won a gold at the 1998 World Championships, the 2004 Stanley Cup, and then the Olympic gold medal in 2006.

Modin still remembers what was going through his mind on June 7, 2004, when the Lightning finally won it all.

"To win the Stanley Cup after such a long grind, it was hard to explain what it feels like. It was a grind, both physically and mentally." After finishing first in the Southeast Division, the Lightning started the playoffs on April 8 against the New York Islanders. After beating New York in five games, the Lightning swept the Canadiens before moving on to face the Philadelphia Flyers.

"We went to a game seven against the Flyers in the Conference Final, prior to going to a seven-game series with the Flames. I was on the ice for the final shift of the Cup Final when the buzzer went off at the end of the game. I was extremely happy for all of us, for reaching a goal we had dreamt of since we were kids. It was a feeling of relief and total happiness. We were so drained—you don't realize you are a Cup champion until a couple days afterwards during all the celebrations."

Modin's day with the Cup was towards the tail end of a wild European tour that summer. The Cup had already paid a visit to Russia, to the Czech Republic, and then to Slovakia before making its way to Sweden.

"I got the Cup in July 2004. I know the Cup had come from Slovakia before it got to my hometown of Sundsvall, Sweden. The Keepers of the Cup came in the afternoon, and they were worn-out. Mike Bolt and his partner Walt [Neubrand] from the Hockey Hall of Fame were tired from the previous visits.

"We had two players from the Czech Republic and one from Slovakia and they were a bit younger than me. I got the feeling that Mike and Walt didn't feel comfortable leaving the Cup out of their sight during their time there. Once they arrived, we took the Cup to the rink I started playing hockey in Sundsvall, the Njurunda Sports Club. We held an open house for anyone who wanted to stop by and get a picture with the Cup. We had a lot of people who came through town that day to take a picture with the Cup. Everyone involved with the Njurunda Sports Club had organized a great setup for the event. I signed autographs for a few hours while people got photos with the

Cup. From there, we took the Cup to our cottage in the Sundsvall area. We had some friends and family come over to take some pictures.

"After a while, the Keepers of the Cup, Mike and Walt, were ready for bed," Modin continues. "They also recognized it was a little early in the evening to take the Cup away from me and my family. They asked me if I could be trusted with the Cup. They really wanted to know my plans for the night. I told them we didn't have anything planned beyond having some friends and family come over and hang out with the Cup. They went back to their hotel and left the Cup with me overnight. The two of them desperately needed to catch up on some sleep.

"While they slept, we took pictures with the Cup throughout the evening. The Cup was very safe that night. It rested between my wife and me as we slept.

"The next day, Mike and Walt came out to the cottage early to start the day. It is a good thing they got some sleep, because it was the biggest day we had planned. We had a big party at the cottage. We had friends and family and neighbors coming by. It was a cool day. We had some drinks and enjoyed the Cup with my buddies and other people who lived around the same lake as me."

Modin was happiest sharing his day with others.

"It was fun to see how people reacted when they saw the Cup. Some of them were really excited. There were some people who I didn't think knew much about the Cup and what it was all about, and even those people were excited to be near it. To hold it and touch it and to take pictures with the Cup made a lot of people incredibly happy. I am really happy that the first thing I did with it was share it with the community and my sports club. My biggest goal that day was to hang out with the Cup, and we also wanted to make sure that we got to do what we wanted.

"I think a lot of people in Sundsvall appreciated that. It wasn't too crazy showing it off. We took time with it and shared it with the people that meant a lot to me. Having the Cup felt like having an extra buddy hanging out with you for the entire day."

During some quiet time, Modin did what everyone else does: he searched names.

"When I had some alone time with the Cup, I went through some of the names on it. I got down to the legends of the game, and to see their names on it, that is a cool thing for me. The alone time I was able to have with it, that was my favorite experience of spending a day with the Cup. When I looked through the names on the Cup it hit me—my name is on there too. That connection is an incredible honor to me."

Looking at photos from his day with the Cup brings instant happiness to Modin.

"That whole Cup experience was unique. Anytime that I see a picture from either one of those days, it brings back good memories. It also reminds me of the grind of what it took to be a Cup champion and have a chance to have a day with it. Every time I see a photo of myself with the Cup, it brings a big smile to my face. Every time I watch the playoffs and I see the Stanley Cup being awarded, it brings back memories of winning the Cup in 2004, for sure. I watch the Cup being awarded and right away I think, *I won it too!*"

Modin didn't care what he drank, as long as it was from the Cup.

"We drank a lot of champagne and beer. And yes, it always tastes better when you drink it out of the Stanley Cup!"

The parties were fun, but to Modin, the quiet times with the Cup meant the world to him.

"I am so glad we didn't plan too many public outings when I had the Cup. I felt like we did it right. It gave me a chance to cherish the Cup and what it means to me. When the Cup was in our bed with my wife and me, that was a great moment. I felt the spirit of the game and the power of the Cup.

"There is usually so much noise when the Cup goes anywhere. People get excited; they want to talk to you and take pictures. But when you are alone with the Cup, it feels different. All the names of the players and the teams that are etched on the Cup and suddenly they are hanging out with you, and only you. And knowing that your name is on there too is a powerful feeling."

A Hall of Fame Proposal

André Roy isn't known for his big shot or his goal-scoring abilities, but he played a key role in the Lightning's run to the Stanley Cup in 2004. His even being there is a testament to his will and dedication to the game.

While Freddy Modin never played a game in the minors, Roy paid his dues in the minor leagues for the first four years of his pro career. Roy's role on whatever team he played on was no secret: he was a big man who was there to provide a physical presence on the fourth line.

"My last year of major junior hockey was a great year for me. I was nineteen years old, and I was coming back from training camp with the Boston

Bruins. I started the year with Chicoutimi, and I had a lot of confidence. I was traded to Drummondville at the end of the season and finished strong."

Once his junior hockey days were over, Roy started grinding it out in the minor leagues. "I spent three years in Providence in the AHL. I ended up playing twenty-odd games in the ECHL. I went back to Fort Wayne of the IHL and had a good year. By the time I arrived in Tampa, I was slowly establishing myself in the NHL."

When Roy arrived in Tampa, he had spent three seasons with the Ottawa Senators. He was also well aware of what was expected of him.

"I knew that I had prepared myself for my job. Every year I showed up at camp, there were young guys that were pushing you and they wanted your job. I had to work hard, keep pushing, and prepare myself as a player. I fought; I played tough. I also wanted to do more offensively and contribute in any way that I could in the limited role with the team."

Roy arrived in Tampa at the tail end of their dark years.

"When I first arrived in Tampa, we were not too good. During my time in Ottawa, the first two years, we would play the Maple Leafs in the first round of the playoffs. And every year, we lost in the first round. My third year in Ottawa, I had a good year, and we were headed to another playoff run against the Leafs. Then, boom, I got traded to Tampa. Even though we didn't make the playoffs, I had fun playing in Tampa. I got to know the guys on the team, and I fell in love with the area. Living in Tampa, when you are not at the rink, you have golfing, shopping, restaurants, beaches, you name it. Even Disney is within a short drive."

The Lightning were run by one of the toughest coaches in recent memory.

"John Tortorella was our coach, and he is very demanding," says Roy. "He wants to push every individual the best way that he can to get the best out of you as a player. At the same time, we had some star players that were coming into their own. Vinny Lecavalier, Brad Richards, and Martin St. Louis. We also had traded for Danny Boyle the year I arrived. In the 2002–03 season, we made the playoffs, and we made it to the second round before losing to the Devils. Then I looked at our roster at the start of the 2003 season and it hit me. *Man, we might be very good this year.* We believed in each other and believed that we could be a contending team."

While the Lightning were building into something special, the same couldn't be said for Roy's relationship with Tortorella.

"During the regular season, I only dressed for thirty-three games. Torts [John Tortorella] and I had a few screaming matches. I was healthy that whole season and I ended up being a healthy scratch for over forty-five games that year. I was pissed-off, and I think Torts was trying to get me upset so that when I went into the lineup, I would react that way. I am not the type of guy that would go into his office, yell, and scream. That is just not me, that isn't my personality. I tried to stay quiet, I did my workouts, got my rest, and I came to the rink ready to play. But there were times I let him know how I felt.

"Towards the end of the season," continues Roy, "with about ten games left to go, Tortorella pulled me aside and said, 'I know you haven't played a lot this year, André. But I want you to be ready down the stretch. We are going to need you! You will be important and a big factor. We need your energy and your physical presence.' Torts said to me that he was going to rotate the four guys who made up the fourth line. There was always one guy who sat out during the regular season. At the start of the playoffs, he told me, 'Be ready, I am going to need you.' Just hearing that made me feel good.

"I always needed a coach that was open to what he needed from me and what he wanted from me," says Roy. "I wanted a coach that made me feel important even though I had limited ice time. When

Torts told me that he needed me, I had a boost of confidence. I ended up dressing for twenty-one games in our Cup run and I played my best hockey of the year. I scored a goal in our first game against the Islanders, and I played well against the Habs and the Flyers. We beat the Flyers in seven games, and I played an important physical role. I fought Donald Brashear. Against the Flames in the Cup Final, I played the first five games. I ended up being a healthy scratch in game six and seven."

Tortorella mixed up the lines even further. "Before game five, Cory Stillman was playing okay. Torts sat him out and he brought in Ben Clymer. Clymer hadn't played the whole playoffs before that. Clymer had a strong game in game five and then Torts brought Stillman for game six. Since Clymer played so well in game five, Torts kept him in the lineup for game six and then I was told I wouldn't be playing. After twenty-one games in a row, Torts told me at the morning skate that I wasn't playing.

"He told me, 'André, right now, this is the decision I took. We are not going to argue over this, that's my decision.' I stayed quiet, expecting to dress for game seven. Then at the morning skate of game seven, Torts told me, 'We are going with the same lineup as game six.' I was upset. He told me, 'André, this is not about you right now. This is about the team.' I swallowed my pride and got in my car and drove home. I was so mad and sad at the same time.

"I called a good friend of mine back home in Quebec and he said to me, 'Do you know what, you deserve to win the Cup just as much as anyone on that team. You contributed to the team, so you go out there and do your thing. You are a big part of that team.' I said to him, 'You know what, you are right.' So, I went out and bought a camcorder to record everything that night. I wanted to remember everything from that night. After the game ended and we won the Cup, I went out there and celebrated on the ice. After all the ups and downs in my career, from minor hockey to junior hockey to the ECHL, it hit me: *Man, I finally made it.*

"When you see the Stanley Cup come out onto the ice and you are with your teammates, I kept thinking, *Wow, my name is going to be on the Stanley Cup.* I thought of all of the sacrifices I went through and that my parents went through and to finally win the Cup, I was truly fortunate to be a part of that Lightning team."

When André Roy had his day with the Cup that summer, he was determined to make the most of every second with it. That included using the Cup to help propose to his wife.

"I had been dating my girlfriend for about four years and I knew that she was the one. A good friend called me during the Cup Final. He used to work for RDS [Quebec's francophone sports network] and he had planned some parties in the past for people like Martin Brodeur. He asked me if he could organize my day with the Cup and I said, 'Sure.' I told him I was thinking of getting married. He looked at me and said, 'You should do it during your day with the Cup.' I wondered if it would be too much all on the same day. He said, 'Why not?' I thought about it, and I agreed. 'Why not, indeed?' I went out and bought an engagement ring and I decided to do it.

"The day the Cup arrived, the Keeper of the Cup arrived at my house in Blainville, Quebec, just outside of Montreal. I spent two hours there, taking pictures of the Cup with my family. My mom and dad were there as well as my brothers. It was fun and a couple of neighbors stopped by. From there, I went with the Cup to the golf course by my house. A helicopter was waiting for me, and my pilot was Guy Lafleur! I didn't even know, but Guy Lafleur had a license to fly helicopters. When Guy stepped out of the helicopter, I was stunned. 'Guy Lafleur is our pilot?!' He was so nice. 'Hey, how are you doing? Congratulations!' I couldn't believe what was happening. He said, 'Jump in,' and we took off for Saint-Jérôme.

"I watched Lafleur as a kid and couldn't believe he was flying me to my hometown."

Roy's big day with the Cup continued. "During the flight from Blainville to Saint-Jérôme, my girlfriend was with me, and she was looking outside the window. She wasn't sure how she felt about flying in a helicopter. I put the ring in the Cup. I asked her, 'Do you want to drink out of the Cup? We will pour some booze in it.' She kept looking outside and said, 'No, I am good.' I was pleading with her, 'Take a look in the Cup.' She still didn't look. I kept at it. 'Look, look in the Cup! There is something in it.' She turned around and grabbed the box and said, 'Oh my God!' When she opened it, I proposed to her. 'Would you like to get married?'

"She said yes and got emotional. It was like something out of a movie."

And that was just the start of Roy's day with the Cup. After the proposal, Guy Lafleur landed the helicopter in Saint-Jérôme.

"It was a quick ride to Saint-Jérôme, maybe twenty minutes at best. We landed on a baseball field and took the Cup to city hall. Saint-Jérôme is where I grew up and played my minor hockey. We did some autograph signings and had a parade in the streets. After that, we took the Cup an hour north to Mont-Tremblant and had a big party with my friend's band. We partied on the roof of this place called the Shack. We stayed there until after three in the morning. The Keeper of the Cup was sleeping by the bar. He was so done. He'd been up all night before with Vinny Lecavalier. After he was done with me, he still had to take the Cup to go see Martin St. Louis. I told him to get some rest.

"It was a fun day, and it goes by so fast. There is so much you want to do and so much that you want to share with the Cup. You are talking to people, taking pictures. The next thing you know, it is one in the morning, and you haven't stopped all day.

"I knew the Cup had to go because it was off to another player, but at the same time, I didn't want the day to end," says Roy. "I wish I could have kept the Cup and kept partying. I love my friends, but my buddies get a little out of hand sometimes. And that happened with the Stanley Cup. Well, alcohol makes you do stupid stuff sometimes. My buddies were hammered, and they had been doing shots all night long. Towards the end of our night in Mont-Tremblant the Cup was sitting on a table. I was talking to everyone, and I wasn't watching the Cup that closely. Walt Neubrand, the Keeper of the Cup, got up and said, 'Hey!'

"One of my buddies had the Cup turned upside down and they were pouring beer into the bottom end of the Cup. Walter freaked, 'You can't do that with the Cup! Respect the Cup, guys!' I could tell my buddies felt bad when I saw their reaction. I told them, 'Don't fuck around with the Cup, guys, have a little respect!'

"They all said, 'Oh, sorry, André, we thought it would be fun.' I looked at them. 'I know, guys, but it is the Stanley Cup.'

"I didn't want the Cup guy to get mad at me. That is what happens when you party that much. It wasn't too bad, nothing got broken. Basically, everyone wanted to raise the Cup over their head. The Keeper of the Cup wouldn't let people do that unless I was holding one side of it. A few times my buddies tried to raise the Cup over their heads by themselves and the Keeper of the Cup looked at them. 'No, you can't do that.' Other than that, it was a good night, and it all went well."

It's hard to believe, but Roy did have a quiet moment with the Cup.

"In the morning, when the Cup arrived and I was with my family, it was pretty quiet. We set the Cup on the table and took pictures. I joined my dad and my brothers, and we were looking at names, especially the Montreal Canadiens of the seventies and the 1986 team with Patrick Roy.

"My favorite photo of my day with the Cup is one that I cherish to this day. I am standing with Guy Lafleur and my good friend Paul Buisson from RDS.

"That photo of the three of us standing together with the Cup is special to me. Both of them have left the earth now. Because of that, that one photo means everything to me.

"I also love the team picture on the ice after we won the Cup, and we are all wearing our Stanley Cup champion hats. We are all gathered together around the Cup with all the support staff, and I am right by the Cup. I told myself that I was going to be in a great spot for this team picture. This picture was going to be forever, and I kneeled down right beside the Stanley Cup, and Torts was on the other side. Whenever I look at that photo, I think of what a fun time in my life that was. Every time that the playoffs start, that is when I miss playing in the NHL so much. Still to this day, whenever I get to see the Cup, I always go and look to see where my name is."

Whenever André Roy is having a bad day, he only has to think about one thing, and he is instantly happy.

"There are a lot of times I will think to myself, *Hey, I won the Cup.* I work at RDS now and Jacques Demers, the former Canadiens coach who won the Cup in 1993, talked to me and he said, 'André, you remember this. You were not just a tough guy. You are a Stanley Cup champion. Be proud, keep your head up, you had a hell of a career.' I often look back on my NHL career and I think, *My name is on the Cup.*

"I don't wear it often, but whenever I get my Stanley Cup ring out and put it on, I start having all these memories of our Cup run in 2004. The whole thing is a dream come true. All players work for and dream of that day, and I was lucky enough to be a part of it."

It's the same dream come true for every champion, but not everyone gets a helicopter ride from Guy Lafleur and a successful proposal to his girlfriend with the Stanley Cup.

CHAPTER 10

May Day Is Finally a Champion

2007 Anaheim Ducks
Brad May

In spring 1993, a then twenty-one-year-old Brad May scored one of the most dramatic playoff goals in the history of the Buffalo Sabres. In overtime, May took a pass from future Hall of Famer Pat LaFontaine, burst past another future Hall of Famer, Ray Bourque, moved in on net, and beat playoff veteran goaltender Andy Moog for the game-winning—and series-winning—goal. The Sabres had swept the mighty Bruins four games to zero.

Rick Jeanneret's iconic call of "May Day! May Day! May Day! May Day! May Day! Brad May wins it in overtime!" still echoes in Buffalo. But their playoff run was cut short when they faced the Montreal Canadiens, losing in four straight to end their Cup dream.

After Buffalo, Brad May bounced around the league from Vancouver to Phoenix, back to Vancouver, and then on to Colorado. More than fourteen years and seven hundred games after that run in Buffalo, May was a journeyman forward, still grinding it out in the NHL. And, it seemed, light-years away from becoming a Stanley Cup champion. At that point, May was nearing the end of his long pro career.

As you might expect, Brad May thought his big playoff moment was just the beginning of something special in Buffalo.

"After I scored that overtime goal and we beat the Bruins, we ended up losing three overtime games to the Canadiens in the next round. I was twenty-one years old, and I thought I would have a perennial crack at going to the Stanley Cup. In some ways, you take it for granted as a young player. All of a sudden, I was in my fifteenth year in the NHL and had gone through a number of playoff series, and I still hadn't won a Cup," says May.

As the years rolled on, the drive to win a Stanley Cup never waned.

"The older I got, my mindset was that I want to play as long as I can. I want to play to make money, obviously, but also to have a chance to try and win the Stanley Cup," says May.

Eventually, doubt crept into his mind.

"I had played on some good teams, and we always fell short of our goal. All of a sudden it is five years later, and you get beat again. Then I started to wonder if it ever was going to happen," said May.

"My fifteenth year in the NHL, I was playing for the Colorado Avalanche, and I dislocated my shoulder in training camp. I then had to undergo shoulder surgery for the fourth time in my career. I was out for five months that year. I knew I was going to come back and get healthy, because I had gone through it before. So, I knew I could get healthy enough to play. But the Avs that year, they didn't even make the playoffs. I did think that if my shoulder didn't respond to therapy and training that my playing career might be over. I always worked hard and would grind every day, but I also realized my window to win a Cup was closing fast," adds May.

On February 27, 2007, May was traded from Colorado to a veteran-laden Anaheim Ducks team. All of sudden, May was on a team that boasted three future Hall of Famers in Teemu Selänne, Chris Pronger, and Scott Niedermayer.

"I had been traded at the trade deadline before in my career, so I anticipated getting dealt that day. Leading up to the deadline, I felt I was auditioning to either stay in Colorado or be picked by another team at the deadline. I wasn't shocked that I was traded, but I didn't anticipate Anaheim at all. After conversations with my agent, I had heard that there were other teams that were interested. One of them was the Ottawa Senators," says May.

"I ended up being traded to Anaheim and reunited with their general manager, Brian Burke. Burkie traded for me twice in my career at the trade deadline. I played for the Vancouver Canucks for a few years when Burkie was the GM."

May arrived in Anaheim and joined a Ducks team that was among the elite of the NHL that year.

"When I arrived at the deadline, the Ducks were in a battle with the San Jose Sharks to finish first in the division and get home-ice advantage in the playoffs. We had some games down the stretch with San Jose that were really energetic and exciting. We ended up winning the division and we had home-ice advantage throughout the playoffs, except for our series with the Red Wings."

Once the playoffs started, Anaheim only lost four games through the first three rounds.

"We won every round that year four games to one, except for the Conference Final with Detroit, which ended up going to six games. By the time we got to the Cup Final, we knew."

Standing in Anaheim's way of winning the Stanley Cup were the Ottawa Senators.

"While there is always some reservation and a little hesitation, we certainly didn't dwell on it," says May. "Before the start of our series with the Sens, we all thought, *We are going to pound this team.* The idea of saying '*If* we win the Cup' was not in our vocabulary that year. Collectively we all believed we would win the Cup, and that made it more powerful. We respected Ottawa, and we knew they were a solid team, but we were self-confident and there was not a chance they would beat us. On our back end we had Scott Niedermayer, Chris Pronger, and François Beauchemin, [who] played the most minutes of any of our defensemen.

"Our third line that year ranks right up with the Bobby Holík, Randy McKay, and Mike Peluso line in New Jersey when they won the Cup. Or even the Kris Draper, Kirk Maltby, Darren McCarty line in Detroit. We had Travis Moen, Sammy Påhlsson, and Rob Niedermayer. They all scored goals and produced offense, and they all shut down the best lines of every team we faced. They were just awesome. The three of them should have collectively won the Conn Smythe Trophy, they were that good. We had just a wonderful team and a wonderful group of guys."

The 2007 Ducks overcame numerous hurdles that few people knew about.

"We had a lot of adversity throughout the playoffs that people don't really understand. Going into the playoffs, Ilya Bryzgalov was the starter [in goal], and he was great those first three games against the Minnesota Wild. He stood on his head those first few games and it is a good thing he did, because Minnesota had a solid team that year.

Then J.-.S Giguère took over as the starting goalie. He was injured going into the playoffs and then he had to deal with some personal stuff involving his newborn son. Chris Kunitz was injured twice during the playoffs. I played most of the playoffs with a broken hand. Chris Pronger ended up having shoulder surgery at the end of the playoffs. In game three against Minnesota, François Beauchemin took a puck in the face and broke his jaw. He wanted to play in game four, and they wouldn't let him. He ended up playing the rest of the playoffs with a broken jaw. Unknown players like Ryan Shannon and Aaron Rome and Drew Miller and Joe Motzko would come up from the minors and play important minutes. Chris Pronger was suspended twice in the playoffs. Ric Jackman filled in one night and he scored a goal. Joe DiPenta was in and out of the lineup and filled in for Pronger in game four of the Cup Final and was solid."

On June 6, 2007, before a rabid crowd at Anaheim's Honda Center, Brad May and the Ducks beat the Senators in the fifth game of the series to become Stanley Cup champions. After the celebrations and the parade, general manager Brian Burke talked to the players about what to expect that summer.

"Brian Burke let all of us know when we would get the Cup and how it was going to travel that summer. Burkie really respected the Hall of Fame and the Keepers of the Cup and the challenge they have. He said, 'Here is the deal, guys. As we celebrate with the Stanley Cup and it comes to your house there are two rules, and they are nonnegotiable. One, the Stanley Cup will never go into a casino. And two, the Cup will not go to any strip clubs. You have to promise me that.' We were all fine with those rules. But considering some of the urban legends you hear about the Cup, I understand why he said that. Getting the Cup for a day is a heavy responsibility, and one that as a player, you don't take lightly," said May.

"In the planning, the Cup made its way to Ontario in August. I got my day with the Cup on August 16, 2007. It went from Ric Jackman's place, then to Shawn Thornton's place. From there, the Cup came to me. After I had the Cup, it was heading up north to Sudbury with coach Randy Carlyle. I was very lucky, I ended up having the Cup for almost two full days. Around seven thirty in the morning on Tuesday, August 14, one of the Keepers of the Cup, Mike Bolt, showed up at my grandmother's house in Markham, Ontario. My mom was living with my grandmother and when the Cup arrived, we had Tim Hortons coffee with some Timbits and donuts. I was there with my wife, my kids, and my grandmother. From there we went to my grandmother's church, to share it with all of her friends. That was at the Anglican church in Markham. We had a church social with the Cup. Then we drove the Cup up to my father's house, just off of Coppinwood Golf Club, in Goodwood, Ontario. My dad has a beautiful house on the golf course. My dad and I used to own the land and we designed the golf course. From my dad's house, we took the Cup into Stouffville and started on the east side of town.

"We had a small parade with eight to ten cars and around three or four thousand people lining the street," May continues. "After the parade we visited the York Regional Police Safety Village off Stouffville Road in Bruce's Mill Conservation Park.

"We had another parade in golf carts for all the youth hockey players from Markham and Stouffville. There had to be over fifteen hundred kids there that day. Frank Scarpitti, the mayor of Markham, even declared it 'May Day' on August 16.

"Around three thirty, we drove the Cup to the Duchess of Markham, a classic English pub in Markham. My brother told everybody that we would be there that afternoon and evening. It ended up like a Markham high school reunion and we met so many amazing people. If you couldn't make it to the Duchess, at nine we took the Cup to a bar called Crossroads on Main Street in Stouffville.

"We got there," says May, "and the place was jammed. We had the Cup there until after one a.m. I had rented a bus and we hopped on it with a bunch of people and headed up to my cottage in Muskoka. When we got up there, we went directly to the Lake Joseph Club. My neighbors at the cottage, Russ Grant and Steven Wise, both have helicopters. Steve gave me his helicopter for the day. It is painted black and silver, and he had a Stanley Cup decal added on both doors of the helicopter and the words 'May Day' on the tail. At eight thirty the next morning we took off. The NHL Network came up to the cottage that day and they rode in Russ's helicopter. I had a photographer with me and the Cup in the other helicopter. So, we had photos and videos from both angles.

"We took the Cup to a golf course that I was a member of called Oviinbyrd. We landed on the eighteenth fairway and had some coffee and donuts for some of the members. We got back on the helicopter and flew over Port Carling and on to Bracebridge. We paid a visit to my longtime trainer, Andrew Urban. He was an elderly Polish man, and he was my trainer for over ten years. He was one of the greatest people I have ever met, and I would work out in the back of his house all summer long. We dropped down out of the sky and landed in his side yard and brought the Cup to his gym. We got some photos in his gym and that was special.

"We headed back to the Lake Joseph Club and had some lunch and drinks. Then it was off to the Muskoka Woods kids camp. There were twelve hundred kids at the camp, and they all knew there was going to be a hockey theme. So, all the kids had their hockey jerseys. We landed and all the kids came running over and I arrived with the Stanley Cup.

"While all this was going on, we were raising money for two charities: Autism Speaks and a place called Camp Oochigeas. It is a camp for kids with cancer. We told all the adults that for ten dollars a picture, you could get a photo with the Cup and the proceeds went to charity. We ended up raising around twenty-five thousand dollars that day.

"There were fifty-eight kids at Camp Oochigeas the day we arrived. We spent close to two hours at the camp. That was the best part of the whole Stanley Cup experience, the time we spent with kids at Camp Oochigeas. Out of respect to the kids and their families, we were not allowed to take photos. It is a serene place and when we arrived, the kids made up these camp songs for us and the Stanley Cup. My wife and I were in tears, it was amazing, and the kids were fantastic.

"From there, we went back to Muskoka Woods to get back on the helicopters. On top of everything else that day, MasterCraft boats gave us two boats to use for the day. I got in the boat with the Cup and left Muskoka Woods on Lake Rosseau.

"We stopped at a man's cottage because he has a waterfall. His name is Bobby Genovese," continues May. "Three or four weeks before I had my day with the Cup, I pulled up to his dock. I didn't know him, and he didn't know me. I asked him if on August 16 I could bring the Stanley Cup to his waterfall. Bobby looked at me and said, 'Absolutely!' When we pulled up to his cottage with the Cup, he had about fifty of his friends there for a cocktail party with the Stanley Cup. After all that, we got back to our cottage to relax briefly."

The rest of Brad May's time with the Cup reads like a Hollywood script, including the incredible backstory to his next visit.

"I had a dislocated shoulder earlier that season. During the All-Star break, in January 2007, I went to Naples, Florida. I spent time with a longtime friend, Mike Andlauer. He is [the new] owner of the Ottawa Senators. At the time he owned the Hamilton Bulldogs of the AHL. I was playing golf with Michael DeGroote and Andlauer. Somewhere towards the end of the front nine, I said to Mike Andlauer, 'Hey, how is your team doing?' He told me they were in a playoff spot, and they were battling hard.

"I looked at him and said, 'Well, I haven't played a game all year. I hope to return to the lineup in February. I will tell you what, Mike. If your team wins the Calder Cup and if I come back and somehow win the Stanley Cup, let's share a party.' We shook hands on the golf course to seal the deal.

"Sure enough, the Bulldogs win the Calder Cup and my team, the Ducks, won the Stanley Cup. Well, a deal is a deal, and so we shared a party. You can't make that stuff up! Joining us at the party was Don Lever, one of my old coaches in Buffalo, and Maple Leafs legend Wendel Clark. We went to the Lake Joseph Club and had a wonderful time. There were well over two hundred people there that night. There were friends, family, hockey players, you name it. It was the highlight of the summer. The party went well past three in the morning. The party was still going on, but I was dead. I had the worst headache ever from all that drinking and taking so many photos with the Cup.

"Our cottage is a few hundred yards from the Lake Joseph Club," says May. "I looked at Mike Bolt from the Hall of Fame and said, 'I'm taking the Cup, going home, and going to bed. I will see you at six thirty in the morning.' Mike had to load the Cup and take it up to Sudbury the next day. I took the Cup back to the cottage and locked the door to the master bedroom and slept with the Stanley Cup until six thirty in the morning. My wife came up later and ended up sleeping in another bed with her sister.

"I got up and my wife and I washed and polished the Cup and then I helped Mike Bolt. I drove him to meet the other guys. I said goodbye to the Cup, and it was off to Sudbury and Randy Carlyle.

"I ended up spending just under forty-six hours with the Stanley Cup and I maybe slept four hours in that time. I just didn't want to waste a minute with the Cup. I realized that if I had ever won the Cup a second time, I would have carved out around two hours just to be alone with the Cup with my family. It was busy and amazing, and I felt it was too important to be selfish and I needed to share the Cup with everybody."

And that included his own kids.

"There is a kids' camp near our house and the bar. My kids had around twenty-four of their friends over for a sleepover at the camp near the cottage. At some point in the evening, we brought the Cup over to the camp so they could get some time with it. All the kids ended up eating cereal and ice cream sundaes out of the Cup."

Eventually, Brad May actually had some time to sit down and take a long look at the trophy.

"I looked at a lot of names on the Cup when I had a moment. I pride myself on understanding the history of the game and the players involved. Wayne Gretzky was the first name that I looked for. He was the first player that I was really enamored with as a kid, and I was thrilled to see his name on the Cup. Then I saw Paul Coffey's name and he had become a friend of mine over the years.

"Now, when I had my day with the Cup, our names were not on it yet. We started the next season with a series of games in London, England. None of the members of the Anaheim Ducks saw our names on the Cup until we were in London. We were on a double-decker bus, and it took us to the silversmith that actually made the original Stanley Cup. This little silversmith shop in London, England, is still there, and we watched them etch our names on the Cup.

"Three months after I was with the Ducks in London," says May of an exhibition game, "it was Christmastime. I had broken my foot about a week earlier in practice. I was off rehabbing and trying to stay in shape. Then the team asked me to meet Mike Bolt from the Hockey Hall of Fame early in the morning on New Year's Day. They sent a limo to my house in the Orange County community of Corona del Mar at two thirty in the morning. The limo picked me up, then it picked up Mike Bolt and then someone else from the Ducks. The next thing I know, I was on the city of Anaheim float in the famous Rose Bowl parade. I hung out with the Stanley Cup on the float in the Rose Bowl parade the entire day. To the best of my knowledge, that was the only time that the Stanley Cup was on the Rose Bowl parade. The parade lasts almost five hours, and I lost count how many times that I lifted the Cup over my head so the crowd could take photos as we passed by."

Brad May started playing in the NHL in 1991 and he played his final game in the 2009–10 season. Throughout all of those years and over one thousand games in the league, there is one thing that still humbles him every time he thinks about it.

"I get speechless when I think that my name is on the Stanley Cup. Winning the Stanley Cup was the greatest personal achievement of my life. Winning the Cup was, and it will always be, our legacy as players. Outside of my wife and kids, winning the Cup is the greatest thing that I have ever achieved. We reached the Mount Everest of hockey and we got to the top. To do it as a team is the greatest thing ever and all of us have a bond for life because of it.

"If you look at some of the great dynasties in hockey, the Canadiens, the Islanders, the Oilers, and teams like that, it is a lot of the same names on the Cup during those years. Out of all the guys that have played in the NHL, there are very few names on the Cup. I am forever blessed and honored that I am one of those names. I know this: none of the players that are on the Cup take it lightly or take it for granted."

Having your name on the Stanley Cup is one thing. Sharing that experience with others was even more important to Brad May and his family.

"Our family often reflect back on that day and everything we did with the Cup. It was such a happy family moment for us. When we leave this earth, which we all will at some time, I have one question for you: What's the only thing that you can take with you when you die? The only thing you can take with you when you die is what you gave.

It doesn't matter how much money you have or what kind of car you drive. It is what you gave to other people, because they will live on with your memory. I know that day our family had with the Stanley Cup, we were able to give a lot to others, and that means a lot to me."

True words from a player who never passed up an opportunity to share his success with others.

CHAPTER 11

The Pride of Nova Scotia

2009 Pittsburgh Penguins
Sidney Crosby

Sidney Crosby is the most accomplished player of his generation. He is the winner of three Stanley Cups and multiple gold medals on the international hockey stage—and who can forget the "Golden Goal" that won the 2010 Olympics for Team Canada? He could live anywhere in the world, but after every season, he always comes back home to his beloved Nova Scotia.

And forget about five-star restaurants—true to his Nova Scotia roots, Crosby loves nothing more than grabbing something to eat at a well-known truck stop near his offseason home.

"The Big Stop off the highway is ten minutes from my place. I fill up there and sometimes I get the classic Big Stop breakfast. That is where my buddies and I always meet on road trips."

After finishing grade nine at a junior high in Cole Harbour, Crosby left Nova Scotia for grade ten at Shattuck–St. Mary's prep hockey school in Minnesota. From there he spent his last years of high school in Rimouski, Quebec, while playing junior for the Océanic. Through it all, Crosby's love of his home province never wavered. He is deeply proud to be one of the Nova Scotians who overcame the odds and made it to the NHL.

"There is a certain level of pride coming from Nova Scotia. Growing up, we were always the smaller province. We would go to these travel tournaments, and we were the underdog all the time. I am still proud to represent Nova Scotia.

"I remember as a kid looking up to Al MacInnis and Glen Murray and Cam Russell. I remember and I appreciate how much influence and impact people here in Nova Scotia had on me, whether it was local coaches or teams I played on. I always keep that in the back of my mind. The reason for that is all the NHLers from our province that I mentioned did such an excellent job of giving back and being good role models. I always wanted to follow in their footsteps that way, whether it was the Nova Scotia work ethic or the way that they treated people or the kind of teammates that they were. Those are all things that stand out to me, and it was a path that I wanted to follow. There is a lot of great examples of that, and I want to do my best to try and maintain that legacy as a Nova Scotian."

Coming out of junior, the Rimouski Océanic star went first overall to the Pittsburgh Penguins in the 2005 NHL entry draft (thanks to the mother of all draft lottery wins). In his third season in the league, Crosby and the Penguins lost in the Cup Final to the Red Wings in six games. The very next year, in 2009, Crosby and the Penguins faced the same Red Wings in the Stanley Cup Final. It wasn't the rematch that had him on a mission to win it all; there was something else driving him.

"If you would have told me in 2008 that the next year we would go back to the Final, I would have been motivated," says Crosby. "But losing the Stanley Cup stung so much and I felt like it was such a missed opportunity. I was young and playing with older guys and they were saying how hard it is to even get to the final. I was still young, but the pain of losing, I took that to heart. The next year, our mentality was to learn from that loss the year before. We felt that our team wasn't that much different, but our mentality was just right. We had a lot of respect for Detroit going into the final, but not too much. We also had a better idea of what it would take to win the Stanley Cup. It still took us to game seven to do it, but we made it."

In spring 2009, the twenty-one-year-old Crosby became the youngest captain in the history of the NHL to win the Stanley Cup as the Penguins beat Detroit in seven games.

"Every kid's dream is to play in the NHL and win the Stanley Cup. I was trying to remind myself that as much as I didn't want to put too much pressure on myself, I also understood that winning the Cup is not something that is going to happen every year. We went to the Cup Final in back-to-back years, and you think it is going to be a common thing. But it is not, and you have to remind yourself about that. And since I was only twenty-one years old when I won my first Cup, that is a hard thing to understand. Fortunately, we had some older players who really helped me. Players like Billy Guerin, Hal Gill, Philippe Boucher, and Sergei Gonchar. Not only did they teach us valuable lessons, but they also took the pressure off us and told us to enjoy the moment as well."

Once the celebrations in Pittsburgh died down, Crosby couldn't wait to bring the Cup back home to Nova Scotia.

"I took the Stanley Cup to Cole Harbour, Nova Scotia, and had a parade there," says Crosby. "I took it around to as many places as possible. I took it to the rink that I played my minor hockey. I took the Cup to the veterans' hospital because my aunt used to work there. I did some school projects growing up and I interviewed veterans who were in the hospital. I had a connection to it, the IWK Health Centre, and I wanted to connect with as many people as I could. I also had time with the Cup at my parents' house with the family. It is amazing to see the attention that the Cup gets, wherever it goes. It is a magnet; it attracts people who are not even hockey fans. Everyone is in awe of it; it is a unique thing. When you win the Stanley Cup, you don't realize how many people are touched by it.

"You win the Cup and you have accomplished something, and you have these great memories. But then you have your day with the Cup, and you get to share it with so many people and can see the impact that it has. Your day with the Cup allows you to bring everyone together. That is something you appreciate even more as you spend time with it."

For Crosby, sharing the Cup meant setting up the ultimate game of road hockey with his friends.

"When I had my day with the Cup, I got my childhood friends together and we all played road hockey. Growing up, we had different spots in Cole Harbour where we would play, like a tennis court. A friend of mine, a guy named Kielbratowski, when we played on his street, we called it the Kiel Centre. When we played it was always to win an imaginary Stanley Cup. This year, we had the Cup for real to play for! There are not enough hours in the day to do everything that you want with the Cup, but that was a special memory."

Not only is it true that you'll never win the Cup every year, but hockey can be unforgiving in other ways. Between 2010 and 2013, Sidney Crosby only played a total of ninety-nine regular-season games because of injuries. The memories of those injuries and playoff losses were all erased in 2016 as Crosby led the Penguins to another Stanley Cup victory.

"Winning the Stanley Cup the second time was different. The first time, it was everything you dreamed of. Then I went through injuries, and I missed time, and I experienced a lot of disappointment in the playoffs. All of this happened after I went to the Cup Final in back-to-back years at an early age. Winning in 2016 was a different emotion compared to 2009. It was relief, it was joy, and it was appreciation. It felt good. After those years of disappointment, our Cup run in 2016 kind of came out of nowhere. We had a terrible start to the season, and we had a coaching change. That year was a great example of how fast things can turn around. At one point, it felt like things were not going our way and sort of felt like it just wasn't our year. Then everyone found a way, and everyone came together, and we won it all. That was a cool year, considering how things worked out after our horrible start."

In July 2016, Sidney Crosby brought the Stanley Cup back to Nova Scotia.

"The second time I had the Cup, I tried to change things up. I took the Cup to Citadel Hill," a famous Halifax landmark, "in 2009. In 2016, I had some more events planned with my family. We had a golf outing in the morning, then we drove to the Halifax airport to meet the Cup when it arrived. In 2009, there was a military-type ceremony on one of the Canadian navy ships and then we flew over my house with the Cup aboard a Sea King helicopter. In 2016, we were thinking of different things that we didn't know if they were even an option. All of a sudden, they become available. The challenge is spreading them all out and seeing as many people as possible. In 2016, I split my time with the Cup between Nova Scotia and Rimouski, Quebec. I love Rimouski. I played my junior hockey there and it is a place that means a lot to me. I did not expect the turnout that we got when we arrived. But to see how excited people in Rimouski were when we showed up, it was an eye-opening experience."

To Crosby, the only bad thing about having a day with the Cup is being forced to give it back.

"When you have to give the Stanley Cup back to the Keeper of the Cup, it is the worst. In 2017, Mike Bolt was the Keeper of the Cup, and he took the Cup away at the end of my day. I just looked at him and said, 'Really? Do you have to?' I wanted to keep it for another night. But I will say this: you are exhausted when your day is over. I was lucky enough to have it for a day and half one year."

While Crosby went out of his way to share the Stanley Cup with as many people in Nova Scotia as humanly possible, sharing the Cup with his family meant the world to him.

"When I had the Cup at home, I could see the emotions from my dad and my mom, from my sister, and my cousins. I always knew how proud my uncles were of me, but to see their reaction when they saw the Stanley Cup, that was surprising. They played hockey at a high level themselves, but to see how proud they were for me and how much it meant to them to be a part of the celebrations, that meant everything to me. They would cheer me on when I was young and travel to my tournaments and games and they would give me tips. All of those people in my life had a part in winning the Stanley Cup. I wasn't surprised at their emotions, but at the same time, it hits you how proud they were and what it meant to them. To see that is very motivating—to do it again and see their reactions again."

The emotion shown by his family and by everyone else when he shared his day with the Cup is what drives Crosby to work so hard in the offseason.

"You can't really understand how much you want to win a Stanley Cup again until you go through all of the experiences of what it felt like to have the Cup for a day. Spending a day with the Cup and sharing it with others is a combination of joy and happiness, but you also appreciate all the little moments and the little memories that the Stanley Cup provides for you. When you have the Cup for a day, it allows you a chance to connect with so many people who had a part in it too. Winning the Cup is one thing, but it is those moments that stick out just as much."

Crosby loves the history of the game, and he was in hockey heaven as he looked at the names of the other players on the Cup.

"I love looking at names on the Cup. I believe there are sixty years' worth of players' names on the Cup, depending on the number of rings on the trophy at any one time. In 2016, I knew they were about to change one of the rings of names. I remember thinking to myself, *Wow, I am lucky my name is on the Cup at the same time as icons like*

Bobby Orr. I was so lucky to be on the Cup at the same time as these legends of the game, the Oilers dynasty and teams like that. When you take the time to go through it and look at the names on the rosters of teams that won it, it is a great experience. There are some names that are marked out. I believe it was the name of one of the owners' dogs! The dog's name ended up on the Cup somehow, and they crossed it out. I had a good laugh at that. The Stanley Cup is such a unique trophy that way."

Nova Scotia is famous for many things, not least of which is Alexander Keith's beer. So, you know what Sidney Crosby was drinking out of the Cup.

"In 2009 we had an event at the Alexander Keith's brewery in Halifax. Both of my grandmothers drank beer out of the Cup. My one grandmother, I had never seen her drink a drop of alcohol my entire life. But that night, she made an exception for the Stanley Cup. She wasn't going to pass on that one. Lots of Alexander Keith's beer was drunk from the Cup and a little bit of champagne. But my grandmother drinking out of the Cup is something that I will always remember."

Sidney Crosby has a hockey resume most players could only dream of. At the top of his list of accomplishments is the fact that he is a three-time Stanley Cup champion.

"Being a three-time champion means a lot to me," says Crosby. "Because I understand just how tough it is to win a Stanley Cup. You need so many things to go right to win a Cup. On top of that, you need to be a part of a special group of players. There are a lot of great players in the NHL that, for whatever reason, didn't win the Cup. Maybe they didn't get the bounces in the playoffs, or they weren't able to put a long run together. It isn't because they didn't play well, or they didn't work hard; it is none of those things. To win a Stanley Cup, you need some bounces too. You need things to go your way. That is what you appreciate after winning the Cup, just how much it takes and how many people go into winning it. You realize how lucky you are to be a part of it, because there are a lot of players who have done more than enough to win it, but their name isn't on the Cup."

What some people may not know about Sidney Crosby is the role that music played in his three Stanley Cup victories.

"You look at every year in the playoffs, and teams have different songs that become their own. I link certain songs with certain playoff runs over the years. Years down the road I will hear a song and think, *I remember that song—that was what we always listened to in 2009 when we won the Cup!*"

When looking back on his three Stanley Cup wins, there are two photos that stick out to Crosby.

"In 2017, I was taking the Stanley Cup into the dressing room. I was by myself, coming down the hallway, about to go into the dressing room. I was wearing my champions hat and my champions T-shirt. The hallway was empty. I still remember that feeling, when it hit me. *This is so weird.* Usually there are so many people around. That thought was running through my mind as I turned the corner to go into the dressing room. And that's where everybody was, they were all waiting for me! Those pictures are snapshots in my head that will last forever.

"There is another photo of me," continues Crosby, "sitting with my dad and the Stanley Cup by the fireplace at my parents' house. I see that photo and think, *This is what you dream of when you start playing hockey.* Those moments and those snapshots, those are the things that stick with me. I am lucky that I have some cool photos of me with the Stanley Cup over the years. I have some room left, though! I am hoping to get some more photos before I am done playing hockey."

And Crosby certainly isn't done making Nova Scotia proud every time he steps on the ice.

CHAPTER 12

Boston Strong

2011 Boston Bruins
Johnny Boychuk and Rich Peverley

Memories of a Lifetime

Since the 1990s, after every home game win the Boston Bruins play the classic sixties song "Dirty Water" by the Standells for the cheering fans. The song perfectly expresses the pride Bostonians feel about their city. They love it, warts and all, and they *love* their hometown sports teams. And few teams represented their city better than the 2011 Bruins.

At the start of the 2010–11 season, the Bruins were still trying to recover from their epic playoff collapse to the Flyers the previous spring, where after taking a three-game lead they dropped four games in a row in the second round. The Flyers became only the third team in the NHL up until that point to come back from a three–nothing deficit and win a playoff series. It was a collapse so monumental that it was in the thoughts of all the Bruins during the 2011 playoffs.

One of the key players on that team was Johnny Boychuk, a defenseman with a booming shot nicknamed "Johnny Rockets" by

Boston broadcast legend Jack Edwards. Boychuk remembers well the mood going into the 2011 postseason.

"We were coming off the year before in 2010 where we had a three–nothing series lead to Philly and ended up losing to the Flyers in seven games. It left a sour taste in our mouth. And in 2011 we went to a game seven against Montreal in the first round. From there we faced the Flyers again. And we were up three–nothing in the series, again. Going into game four, we all

felt we learned our lesson from the year before and we closed out the series in four games."

Nothing came easy to the 2011 Bruins in the postseason, not even the weather.

"We beat Tampa Bay in the next round. I still remember that series because it was so bloody hot in that arena in Florida during the playoffs. When we beat the Lightning in game seven, I was excited to go to the finals. At the same time, I was so hot, I didn't know what was going on! From there, we went on to Vancouver to face the Canucks in the Cup Finals."

Inside the Rogers Arena in Vancouver, all that Boychuk was thinking about was the Stanley Cup.

"When I lifted the Cup over my head, it was surreal," says Boychuk. "Obviously, it was happening, but at the same time, it was like a dream. For years, as a kid, I would pretend to hold the Stanley Cup over my head when I was playing street hockey or pond hockey. I was always thinking about it growing up. Then to be actually lifting the Cup, it felt so weird. I was doing it, but it almost didn't seem real. My parents were there, my brother was on the ice, all my teammates were there. I was in the dressing room after we won, with my fiancée and my family and there was beer everywhere. I heard that they had to replace all the carpets in the visiting dressing room in Vancouver. It was gross, we made such a mess!

"My parents left to go back home to Edmonton," Boychuk continues. "My fiancée got on the team charter they had for all the wives and girlfriends. The team stayed in the arena an extra three hours. The whole thing was a blur. We finally got on the plane back to Boston around eleven p.m. local time. The riots in Vancouver were so bad we couldn't leave the arena for at least three hours after the end of the game."

Of course, the celebrations continued once they could get back to Boston. Boychuk clears up the legend of the Bruins' $150,000 bar tab they racked up at a team party there.

"The champagne cost one hundred thousand dollars! It was called Ace of Spades. If you look at the bill, it looks outrageous because of that one bottle. But they comped us that champagne."

Before getting his day with the Cup, Boychuk had an incredibly busy summer.

"After we won the Cup, my soon-to-be wife and I went on our stag and stagette. Then we got married and went on our honeymoon. When we got home, I had to start training, at least as much as I could. We finally got the Cup in early August."

He took it to somewhere special in Edmonton.

"My wife and I had a car service to go eat lunch with the Cup, along with immediate family and friends. From there we took the Cup to the Stollery Children's Hospital in Edmonton. We spent at least three hours there. The kids that are in there, they don't have much to be happy about. I remember the times I did hospital visits with the Bruins. By taking the Cup to the Stollery, I felt like I was bringing some joy to those kids. Even the parents, they are often so distraught, they also need some kind of pick-me-up. To this day, I still have people say to me, 'Thanks for bringing the Cup to the Stollery. I was there when you did that. I just want to thank you.' Visiting the Stollery was one of the highlights of my day with the Cup, and it was nice to give back to Edmonton.

"After the hospital, we took the Cup to my house and spent some more time there with family," says Boychuk. "After that, we went to my parents' house. From there, we took the Cup to Sport Edmonton Park. We had close to one thousand people show up, and I stood there the whole time, over three hours, taking photos with everyone who came to see the Cup. The only thing we asked is for people to donate something to the Stollery Children's Hospital. They could donate whatever they wanted, and all the proceeds went to the hospital. After the event at Sport Edmonton Park, I needed to eat something. We headed to a country saloon, Cook County Saloon on Whyte Avenue. My wife and I got there with the Cup; they placed it on the pool table. They put a tablecloth over the pool table to make it look nicer. We left the Cup there and went to grab something to eat at a spot next door. We had to—the entire day was go-go-go, we were on the run everywhere. It felt nice to take a breath and go get something to eat. We were so busy that day, we didn't drink anything until we got to the Saloon. There simply wasn't time until then. We didn't even get to the Saloon till around nine and we didn't eat until ten. It was great to have the Cup, but when we said goodbye, it was almost a relief."

While his family were moved to spend some quiet time with the Cup, being in the presence of it meant more to two other individuals.

"My family was emotional looking at the Cup, but my power-skating instructor and my trainer also got emotional. When I first started in the NHL, I had to work on things, and both of them helped me do that. Along with my family and my wife, my power-skating instructor and my trainer were a big part of my success. I could tell those two guys were getting overcome with emotions looking at me with the Cup."

An avid collector of hockey memorabilia, Boychuk loves to look at photos from that day.

"Anytime I go downstairs to my basement, I have all of my memorabilia and all the trophies that we won that year. I have pictures of the team the night we won. My favorite photo is the one of me and my wife in my parents' backyard with the Cup. There is another one of the two of us with the Cup at the Saloon. She is lifting the Cup, and my wife is just over one hundred ten pounds, and she was struggling to lift it over her head. I was right behind her to help her out!" When the player has their day with the Cup, their family are allowed to lift it, usually under the watchful eye of the Keeper of the Cup. When people drink out of the Cup on that day, the player is supposed to hang on to the Cup and help people get their drink. However, other players in the NHL who haven't won it yet are forbidden from lifting or even touching the Cup.

"We also got this amazing stick picture after we won," Boychuk continues. "After game seven, they took our sticks and cut each stick up into pieces. Whoever played in that final game, a piece of their stick is on the team photo. That is my favorite piece of memorabilia from my hockey career. I look at the picture and it so cool, it always reminds me, 'I actually won a Stanley Cup.' A lot of guys who played in the league for a long time never got a chance to hold the Cup. I was fortunate enough to win and be a part of a team like the 2011 Bruins."

To Boychuk, it was the fans in Boston that made winning the Cup so uplifting.

"During that 2011 playoff run, I don't think I can remember ever hearing a single boo from the Bruins fans. There are other cities you play in where the fans will boo their home team. The best part of playing for the Bruins, it didn't matter who scored, it didn't matter if you got an assist or if you were just on the ice, to the Bruins fans, it was the *team* scoring the goal. The only part of the jersey that matters in Boston is the *B* on the front. At the start of the 2010–11 season, we were in Prague, the Czech Republic, for a series of games. The trainers were putting everyone's jerseys out and they were placing them in the stalls, with all the players' names facing out. I looked at Matty Falconer, our equipment manager, and I asked him, 'Why do you have the names on the jersey facing forward? We have nameplates on our stalls. Why don't you have the jerseys turned around? Isn't it about what is on the front?' He looked at me and said, 'You are absolutely right.' From then on for the rest of the season, when the players went to the stalls, the jersey was turned with the Bruins logo facing to the front. The idea was that it didn't matter what happened, it was all about what was on the front of the Bruins jersey and not on the back. Other than Matty, I don't think anyone else on the team knew the story behind why we did it that year."

Boychuk feels forever connected to the members of that Bruins team.

"To this day, that 2011 Bruins team is special. At the 2022 draft, I saw Rich Peverley and Chris Kelly and Adam McQuaid and Cam Neely and these people who were all a part of our team that year. It is something that we will never forget. And it's something that I would like to do again someday! It is pretty special to think that your name is etched in history as part of the Stanley Cup. I also feel good for all of my teammates that year. We were all so close that year, and we still are."

Boychuk is all about the team, the communal effort. It's thanks to that spirit that Stollery Children's Hospital in his hometown of Edmonton had an unforgettable summer of generosity.

Creating His Own Luck

A humble man, Rich Peverley never could have predicted at the beginning of the 2010–11 season that he would be a Stanley Cup champion. Undrafted after playing at St. Lawrence University, Peverley started his pro career as a member of the South Carolina Stingrays of the ECHL. A great attitude, a love of hockey, and a tireless work ethic resulted in Peverley finally getting his shot in the NHL in 2007 with the Nashville Predators.

Starting in 2008 and up until February 2011, Peverley was a member of an Atlanta Thrashers team that was on its way to missing the

playoffs. But a trade landed him in Boston, and he arrived as the Bruins were in the initial stages of a seven-game winning streak.

"It was an interesting turn of events being traded to Boston," says Peverley. "Up until the Thrashers dealt me to the Bruins, I didn't think I would ever get traded. I went from being a top-six player in Atlanta to the third line in Boston. At the start, it took some time for me to figure out where I fit in on the Bruins. The team was amazing, though—every single player was so welcoming, and the leadership group was the best. I just went in there and tried to be the best player that I could be in the role that I was given. I was lucky to play with some fantastic players in Boston in Chris Kelly and Michael Ryder. We hit it off right away. I might have been just a piece of the puzzle in Boston, but I appreciated the opportunity to play for such a talented team.

"It wasn't just talent that made the Bruins special," continues Peverley. "They were led by some of the most respected players in the league. Atlanta had some good leaders, but then I arrive in Boston, and they have Zdeno Chara and Patrice Bergeron and Mark Recchi, who were not just fantastic leaders but fantastic players. Practices with the Bruins that spring were on another level. The intensity and the focus of preparation was just elite. That's what made our stars great players and that's why our team was so good."

Peverley ended up playing a key role for the Bruins during the 2011 playoffs and scored two goals in game four of the Stanley Cup Finals.

"I played on every single line at some point during that playoff run. Game four of the Stanley Cup Finals was bittersweet. What happened in game three with Nathan Horton getting hurt, a lot of emotions were running through the team at that point. With Horton's injury, I was given the opportunity to play with David Krejci and Milan Lucic right away, and I did my best with it. My first goal was important because it gave us the lead. I took a feed from Krejci, and I was all alone against Roberto Luongo, and I scored. Scoring that goal in Boston, with that crowd, was the most fun and incredible hockey experience I ever had."

After the final whistle in game seven, Peverley did what seemed so unlikely for much of his career: he lifted the Stanley Cup.

"Lifting the Cup over my head, I felt thankful. I was thankful to even have an opportunity to play with such a talented team. I dreamt of winning the Cup, I just never knew if it would be a reality. I started my career in the ECHL and I never had an NHL contract until my third year of pro hockey. I was never drafted, and I just worked my way up every step along the way. To be in the Cup Finals, and then to win game seven in Vancouver, it was the kind of feeling that I will never be able to replicate. To this day, when I think about raising the Cup over my head that night, it makes me emotional thinking of all the work that I put in to get there."

Peverley still smiles when he sees the photo of him holding the Cup in the minutes after they won it all.

"There is a photo of me holding the Cup in Vancouver. The look of jubilation on my face says it all. I had a lot more emotions running through me the night we won than the day I had the Cup."

Once all the team parties were finished, it was time for Peverley to book his day with the Cup.

"I got the Cup in late July 2011," says Peverley. "I didn't care when I had it. I just told them I wanted to do it in Guelph, Ontario, where I grew up. The Cup came to our house in the early-morning hours, and we spent at least two hours with it before we did any public events. I was able to spend some alone time with it and that was fun. I enjoyed looking at names on the Cup. I searched out big-name players in the nineties and early two thousands. I even searched out stars from the eighties. I am a hockey nut, and even to this day, I like to watch old games and study the history of the game. My parents put a lot of time in and sacrificed a lot of things to help me make it. Seeing the emotions on their face when the Cup was at the house was special. Seeing the emotions on my wife's parents' faces was nice as well."

Peverley wanted to see other people's reactions too, so he took the Cup to a local arena and allowed fans the chance to get a photo with the Cup.

"I wanted to make sure that everyone had an opportunity to have time with the Cup and take a picture. Guelph is small community. Even though the population is around one hundred twenty thousand people, you end up knowing so many. There were so many great people and friends and family and teachers that helped me over the years, I just wanted everyone to enjoy it. That was the main goal when I had my day with the Cup: I wanted everyone to enjoy it as much as I was. All those people put in so much work to help me and guide me. It was a wonderful day to say thank you to all of them."

Peverley had a bit more planned for his special day.

"We had a band that played at my wedding, and they performed at our Stanley Cup party, and it was a lot of fun. That was the best feeling, listening to the band, seeing everyone drinking out of the Cup and having a fun time. That night will stay with me for a long time. We made sure we had a lot of beer on hand from Wellington brewery, a local brewery in Guelph, to drink out of the Cup.

"Giving the Cup back was tough!" says Peverley. "The Keeper of the Cup showed up at midnight to take it away and move on to the next place. It was in the middle of my party with the band and the beer, and everyone was having a great time. The next thing I know, the Keeper of the Cup packed up the trophy and left. People started trickling out after that. I think it is amazing that in the NHL we get to spend a day with the Stanley Cup after you win. It gives you a chance to appreciate all the time and hard work you put into your career.

Peverley is forever grateful for being part of the 2011 Boston Bruins.

"There are times that I do realize there are a lot of tremendous players out there who never had the opportunity to win the Stanley Cup. I am forever thankful that I had the chance to play with good players to allow me to have my name on the Cup. I think about legends like Marcel Dionne and Jarome Iginla and all these fantastic players who never won a Cup and have those feelings that come with it.

"I had my playing career cut short for health reasons and I still work in hockey as a player development coordinator for the Dallas Stars," Peverley adds. "The longer I work on the management side of hockey, the more I want to experience being a Stanley Cup champion again. Every spring, I get the urge to win again."

There are people who might say Rich Peverley is lucky to be a Cup winner. But those who really know him and know his story understand that if you love something as much as he loves hockey, anything is possible.

CHAPTER 13

"This Is Indian Land"

2012 Los Angeles Kings
Jordan Nolan

Jordan Nolan with his brother, Brandon (*left*), and his father, Ted (*right*)

Today, Jordan Nolan is perhaps best known for his role on the TV show
Shoresy, in which he plays one of the three "Jims" who make up Jared
Keeso's wild, fictional senior hockey team, the Sudbury Bulldogs. But
before TV fame, Nolan was a Stanley Cup champion, and that's how
the people of Garden River, Ontario, know him. Thanks to Nolan and

the Los Angeles Kings, in the summer of 2012 the people of Garden River got a day they will never forget.

Located outside Sault Ste. Marie, Garden River First Nation reserve came to be in 1850 after the signing of the Robinson Treaty. Before then, there was no such place as Garden River. As their website says, traditionally "the Ojibway-Chippewa-Algonquin Indians controlled a vast area of land stretching from the Atlantic Coast to the foot-hills of the Rocky Mountains."

The Nolans have a proud hockey history. Jordan and his brother Brandon both played pro, and their father, Ted Nolan, was an NHL coach of the year. They proudly call Garden River home. A great number of Jordan's family still live there, and they spend quite a bit of time there in the summer.

Jordan Nolan's chance to win a Cup came relatively early in his career. After spending most of his first two seasons in pro hockey in the AHL, he was called up to the LA Kings in February 2012 and he never left. At the age of twenty-two, in his rookie year, he was playing in a heated playoff race. Jordan was called up and ended up playing twenty-six games with the Kings before the start of the playoffs.

"I was so young when I was called up," says Nolan. "I didn't realize near the end of the season that we were two points out of the playoffs, and we needed those wins. I was just happy to be there and to be a part of a great team and a great group of guys. We had a lot of special players on that roster. Going into the playoffs, I was just excited to be in the NHL and I was just taking it day by day."

The team clearly liked his play. Nolan ended up playing all twenty games in the playoffs.

"We had a great fourth line that year. Colin Fraser was our centerman. Kyle Clifford was our one winger. Then Clifford got hurt and Brad Richardson took his place. Darryl Sutter and the coaching staff put a lot of faith in me, and I tried to play with as much energy and physical play that I could. That was my goal, and to make some noise with contact and puck possession down low."

That faith was rewarded in game one of the Cup Final when Nolan set up Colin Fraser on the game's first goal in what turned out to be a 2–1 win over the Devils. On June 11, Nolan and the LA Kings beat the New Jersey Devils in six games to win the first Stanley Cup in the history of the franchise. Nolan was so locked in on doing what he was told, he almost forgot about the magnitude of the moment at the Staples Center in Los Angeles.

"Darryl [Sutter] was a demanding coach, and he expected a lot from his players. We were up six to one late in the third period and Darryl put our line out there to finish the hockey game. I got the puck on the half wall, and I still worked my hardest to get the puck across the blue line. Once I had the puck," continues Nolan, "I chipped it out like I was making a regular play to get the puck out of our zone. I never even thought about picking up the puck at the end of the game! After the game, Luc Robitaille came up to me and said, 'Where's the puck? What did you do with it?' I was so scared of turning it over at the blue line, even though the score was six to one, I still chipped it out. When the buzzer went at the end of the third period, that is when it hit me that we had won the Stanley Cup."

In a unique twist on the usual postgame ritual, Nolan and his Kings teammates had some rare quiet time with the Cup that night.

"After we won, we cleared the dressing room of friends and family pretty quickly. We just had the team in there with the Cup for a good portion of the evening," says Nolan. "I was sitting there with a couple of the guys and started looking at some of the past teams that had won."

Like any pro sports team that wins a championship in Los Angeles, Nolan and the Kings received the full Hollywood treatment.

"In the days after we won the Cup, the Kings held a couple of parties in Los Angeles. David Beckham came out and joined us. Kevin

Connolly from *Entourage* spent time with us. Colin Hanks, Tom's son, came out to the party as well. Tom Arnold was also there. I am a big movie and TV buff, so interacting with them was cool."

Meeting Hollywood actors and A-list celebrities is nice, but Jordan had more important things on his mind.

"Once the playoffs ended, we filled out paperwork, putting in our requests of when we would like the Cup. Right away, I filled out Garden River, Ontario, and picked out my days and times. I got the call a month later and then I started to plan my day with the Cup with my family."

That day came at the end of August. Located fifteen kilometers from Sault Ste. Marie, Garden River is a world away from its larger, more well-known neighbor.

"We are very proud to be Garden River First Nations and we wanted the event to be special for everyone in our community. As well, I knew how much our community supported me all the way through the playoffs. They watched every game at our community center and cheered me on."

Entering Garden River, at the start of the parade for Nolan and the Stanley Cup, there was a sign that read "Ahknee LA Kings."

"*Ahknee* is 'welcome' in our language."

To Nolan, the language and customs and traditions of Garden River were going to be the main themes for his day with the Cup.

"My grandmother, my dad's mom, she used to run the powwows in my community. That got passed down to my aunt Arlene. My dad's parents were very important in his life—unfortunately they passed away when my dad was a young man," Nolan reveals. "My dad's father is named Stan, so we did a traditional sunrise ceremony at the cemetery—my dad said we brought the Stanley Cup to Stan Nolan. Then we did an elders-only ceremony at our community center. The elders are especially important to our community and our culture. So it was important to have an elders-only ceremony with the Cup. After, we had breakfast with them, and they got to take pictures with the Cup. After that, we did a small breakfast at my house with my family. Brandon, my brother, had just had his firstborn, and he came down to watch us in the Conference Final with his then two-month-old son. Brandon and I poured a big box of Lucky Charms cereal into the Cup for breakfast and ate out of it.

"After the private family breakfast," continues Nolan, "we did a parade with the Cup to our powwow grounds. Then we did a traditional powwow where we honored the Stanley Cup, and we did a smudge ceremony with the Cup. This was done to bless the Cup and the whole experience. The smudge ceremony has been used by Indigenous people for thousands of years. It involves the burning of sage or sweetgrass in a small container. The smoke connects us to our spirit or the Creator. The smudge ceremony is also used to bless special objects, such as the Stanley Cup. The whole community got involved that day and a number of other surrounding First Nations communities came around to join in as well. That was important to us. Not just a photo op or signing a few autographs but holding a traditional powwow ceremony for all of the communities that came."

To cap off this special day, Jordan Nolan and his family took the Stanley Cup to a place in Garden River that has deep meaning to them and everyone in the community.

"It was a special time, and after it was over, we took the Cup and drove to the bridge that has 'This Is Indian Land' painted on the side. My uncle Rick Nolan—who is the fire chief in Garden River—he was the first person to paint that bridge with that message. To be up there on the bridge with the Stanley Cup was a powerful moment for everyone," reveals Nolan. "My dad and my brother joined me on the bridge with the Cup and the whole community gathered around on the highway looking back at the bridge, so they could take photos. The bridge is well-known to us and people often stop and take pictures of it when they are driving through. To have that photo of me with my dad and my brother and the Stanley Cup really meant a lot to our community and our people. We had a wonderful time and took some great photos with the Cup at the powwow. But the photo of the Cup on the 'This Is Indian Land' bridge meant so much to everyone."

Hockey has taken the Nolan family all across North America, but Garden River will always be home.

"Garden River is where we spent summers as a family. Growing up, my dad was busy with hockey, but we always found a way to come back home. Garden River is where I trained over the summer, and I used to run and ride my bike along the highway through the community. Even though we moved around a lot, Garden River has always been our home and I knew right away that I wanted to be there with the Cup."

The Stanley Cup wasn't the only trophy in Garden River that day.

"Ken Hill of Six Nations Lacrosse flew his team to Garden River and brought the Mann Cup with them. So, we had the Stanley Cup next to the Mann Cup," says Nolan of the lacrosse trophy awarded to the top senior men's team. "After the parade, we had a lunch at my family's house and took some more photos. We had some friends over and my dad has twelve brothers and sisters, so as you can imagine, we had a lot of cousins and their friends popping by to see the Cup. We also did a bunch of photos and autographs to help raise some money for the community food drive, with the proceeds going to the Garden River food bank."

Nolan also made sure to pay tribute to his dad's NHL coaching career.

"When the Keeper of the Cup called me to confirm what day he was coming, he asked if he should bring my dad's Jack Adams trophy that he won as coach of the year when he was in Buffalo," Nolan says. "We ended up having the Jack Adams trophy and the Stanley Cup in our house for the day. For me and my dad, to come from Garden

River, a small First Nations community, and to have those two trophies there, it was special. I wanted the family to enjoy the Cup and my friends to enjoy it."

Two years later, Nolan and the Kings won the Stanley Cup again. And just like in 2012, the Cup was going "home."

"When the Kings won the Cup again in 2014, I took it back to Garden River. I did pretty much the same things that I did in 2012. We didn't do the sunrise ceremony, but we made the parade a little bit longer. We still had the powwow and the smudge ceremony. We kept everything in Garden River. The Cup has been in Sault Ste. Marie a couple of times, including Tyler Kennedy in 2009 when he won the Cup with the Penguins. So, we really felt this is our time, this is Garden River's time.

"We really just wanted the Cup in our community for the entire day that we had it," says Nolan. "The second time I had the Cup, it was all about the community and especially the young ones. I wanted them to see the Cup and let them know that it doesn't matter where you come from or how rich or poor you are, if you put a lot of hard work into something, you can accomplish anything."

In 2019, Jordan Nolan was an extra player, a black ace, with the St. Louis Blues. While he didn't dress for any playoff games that year, he did practice with the team throughout the playoffs. Because of that, he was allowed to spend a half day with the Cup that summer when the Blues won. A lot had changed in his life from the first time he won with the Kings in 2012.

"The first time I won the Cup, I was single. The second time, I was engaged to my wife. The third time, I was married with our first child. Since I only had a half day, we made our time with the Cup simple. In Niagara-on-the-Lake, near where my parents live now, we went to a winery. We invited close friends and family and kept it small and intimate. My brother had his oldest kid in the Cup the first time I won.

The second time, he had his second child. The third Cup he had his daughter in there."

Nolan's Cup history is unique in more ways than one.

"The first time I won the Stanley Cup, I played every single game in the playoffs. The second time, I started in the playoffs. Then we fell behind three–nothing to San Jose and the team made some lineup changes. The third Cup, I was the black ace the entire playoffs. I am probably the first guy in NHL history to do it in that order!"

While Jordan is proud to have the Nolan name on the Stanley Cup, there are other things in his life of which he is just as proud.

"I am honored to have my name on the Stanley Cup. I am proud of the career that I had. I was a seventh-round pick that made the LA Kings. I am proudest of the first time I won the Cup in 2012 and playing every single game in the playoffs. It is special considering I worked my way from the OHL, to the ECHL, and to the AHL two years before that. But hockey has brought us so much more than having my name on the Cup or winning awards. We got to work with First Nations communities and work with our hockey schools. That is the work that we do to this day that we are the proudest of."

It's safe to say that the community of Garden River is just as proud of the Nolan family.

CHAPTER 14

Bill Ranford Finds a Home

2014 Los Angeles Kings
Bill Ranford

Bill Ranford and family

Bill Ranford has an impressive resume. He is a four-time Stanley Cup champion, a Conn Smythe Trophy winner, and was the MVP of the 1991 Canada Cup. Today Ranford is a respected goalie coach with the Los Angeles Kings.

Ranford is also a proud air force brat. Military "brats" often spend their childhoods moving all over North America, and beyond, as their parents' careers move them from base to base. His father was a fire-fighter in the Royal Canadian Air Force, which meant a lot of moving around the world as a child. Unlike the vast majority of hockey players who make it to the NHL, Ranford lived what can only be called a nomadic life during his childhood.

Ranford was born in Brandon, Manitoba. From there the Ranford family moved to Canadian Forces Base (CFB) Cold Lake, Alberta, then it was on to CFB Baden, in Germany. After that it was CFB Portage La Prairie, Manitoba. From there the Ranfords moved to the opposite end of the country to live on CFB Summerside, Prince Edward Island. Finally, they ended up in Penhold, Alberta.

Ranford started playing hockey when his father was stationed in Cold Lake, Alberta. The odds of a kid moving around that much and making it even as far as major junior hockey are steep. Despite the fact that his family moved eight times while he was growing up, when Ranford was seventeen, he was a goalie with the New Westminster Bruins of the WHL. His three-year stint in New Westminster made a big impression on Ranford. In 2000, after his long NHL career, playing for five NHL teams, came to an end, he built a house there. He has never left.

Bill Ranford is no stranger to the Stanley Cup. Ranford was a backup goalie for the 1988 Oilers team that won it all, and then in 1990, Ranford was brilliant in the postseason as he led the Oilers to another Stanley Cup victory. His performance was so good that he was awarded the coveted Conn Smythe Trophy as the playoff MVP.

Despite his heroics in the 1990 playoffs, Ranford didn't get to enjoy the victory very much.

"We didn't get any time alone with the Cup in 1990," says Ranford. "At the time, there was no real 'Cup tour' like there is now, so we didn't even think about something like that. The odd guy got time with the Cup because they grabbed it, without putting a thought into it. But it was nothing official," said Ranford.

Most might assume that Ranford was forced to wait over two decades to spend a day with the Cup, but they'd be wrong.

"Prior to 2012, I had an opportunity to get the Cup for half a day. They had brought the Cup out to BC. I am involved with the Co-quitlam Express of the BCHL, and as part of the negotiation process as a part owner, they hosted the league's all-star game in 2004. The way we convinced the Hall of Fame to bring the Cup out was to tell them that I had won the Cup twice with the Oilers and I had never had it. As a result, I ended up getting the Cup for an evening and the next morning as part of the BCHL celebrations."

When Ranford got a quiet moment with the Cup, he looked up certain names.

"When I had my time, I looked at all the goalies that I grew up idolizing. I looked up Ken Dryden, I looked up Chico Resch, who I am related to through marriage. I looked at the greats like Jean Béliveau. Because of Chico, I was an Islanders fan. I looked up players on the Islanders dynasty. I was originally drafted by the Bruins, so I looked up a bunch of Bruins greats. You look at the names and you recognize the history of the Cup, and I thought how crazy it was that my name is on there with them. That event with the BCHL in 2004 was the first time that I saw my name on the Cup. When you win the Cup, you don't see your name on it; that comes later.

"I saw my name on the Cup, and it hit me, my name is on it, and nobody can take it off. Until I am past my time, and they have to remove a ring on the Cup, my name is on there. I even love the old-school way in which they engrave the names on the Cup. There is a silversmith with a special hammer and an engraving tool, and they hammer your name into the metal."

Ranford still smiles when he remembers that Cup-winning team.

"I have special memories with everyone on that 1990 Oilers team. When you go through that process of winning the Cup together, there is something that happens where you are tied in with every single guy on the team. It is a special bond that we will have for a lifetime. I can see any guys from the 1990 team or the 1988 team, and it was like we were together yesterday."

In 2012, as the goaltending coach for the Los Angeles Kings, Ranford was finally going to get his proper day with the Stanley Cup after they beat the Devils in six games.

"After the Kings won, I had them bring the Cup to my hometown of New Westminster, BC. I started off by taking the Cup to my sister-in-law's school. Then I took it to the school my wife teaches at. Later on, we had a big party in our backyard. We drank some beer and champagne out of the Cup. It took twelve or thirteen cans of beer to fill the Cup. I had a friend there who wanted to do that and away we went. That was a fun moment. We put lemonade in the Cup for younger kids that were there. We did a little bit of everything for everybody. That is the neat thing about my day with the Cup: I tried to keep the family and friends gathering pretty intimate.

"And we also did a public function at my old junior rink, the Queen's Park Arena in New Westminster," continues Ranford. "That event was a fundraiser through my family. It was a lot of work organizing that as people could come to the arena and get their picture taken with the Cup. I have a charity called SITV, Stick It to Violence. It is a hockey program through my wife's school, and we used the money to help pay for ice time and hockey equipment. It was a wonderful way to give back to the community as people were able to come out and see the Cup. The staff at Queen's Park Arena did an excellent job setting up the platform for the Cup and curtained off certain areas—it was well organized. That's what I love about a small community like New Westminster; everybody was involved with my day with the Cup."

Ranford was moved to see the impact the Stanley Cup had on people.

"At the public event, people are excited to see the Cup. However, the place that I really noticed the impact of the Cup was when we had our own private gathering with family and friends. There were these intimate moments where family and friends would start hovering around the Cup and start looking at names of players they grew up watching. At the arena, people got up there quick, got a photo, and moved on so the next person could get their photo. When the Cup is sitting there in your backyard and people get the time to study it and see the history of it—that is where I was really amazed by the power of the Cup."

He came up with another fun way to share the Cup.

"One of the neatest things that we did with the Cup took place in 2014, the second time that I had the Cup," remembers Ranford. "We were the first people to take the Cup to the famous Roxy nightclub in Vancouver. The Roxy is a spot in downtown Vancouver that NHL players have gone to for years. Milan Lucic took the Cup to the ropes outside the club, but I was the first one who planned an event inside the club. We planned a quiet night at the Roxy early in the week. We took the Cup into the bar and had it up onstage. I had a friend that worked there and the staff and management at the club were about to have a meet-and-greet with the Cup. Nobody outside of my friends had any idea what was going on. The management called a big staff meeting and then they showed up, and all of a sudden, there was the Stanley Cup there for them to take pictures of. We had it up onstage, and at the end of the night, we took it out the back door and went back home.

"That was it for me. By that point, I was done," says Ranford. "It was a long day! But it's cool to think I was the first person to bring the Cup into the Roxy. A couple of the waitstaff at the club had just started working there and I overheard them say, 'Oh my God, do things like this happen every year?' I laughed and told them this is a one-off."

Taking the Stanley Cup to a nightclub is one thing, but spending time with his family and kids was far more important to Ranford.

"When I won the Cup as a player, my kids were not born yet. In 2014, my youngest child and my wife were both able to be in the arena the night we won the Cup. It was pretty crazy, having them both on the ice with me, celebrating with the Stanley Cup."

Once again, Ranford was amazed at the power of the Stanley Cup when he shared it with family and friends.

"A friend of ours, Leslie McQueen, she was absolutely fascinated by the Cup. That blew me away. I didn't know she was as big a hockey fan as she was. She sat in the back corner and anytime that the Cup was left on its own, she was right up there, looking at different names on the Cup. I would have never expected that from her. That moment was pretty cool.

"I loved being able to take photos with family," Ranford reflects. "In 2014, my nephew was with the Texas Stars, and we were able to arrange that both Cups were there that day, the Stanley Cup and the Calder Cup. When we had the Cup with our family and friends, everyone had their own special intimate moment. You could sit back and just watch all day long, observing all the different reactions as people get their time with the Cup."

That included a connection to Ranford's life as an air force brat.

"My dad was in the RCAF in Canadian Forces Base Baden, Germany, and Mr. George Ryan, my grade-seven teacher from Germany, lives in New Westminster. For him to come over to the house and spend part of the day with us was pretty cool. Anytime a friend gets to see the Cup, it means a lot. Sometimes you forget the magnitude of the Cup, until you witness other people around it. Then it really hits you what the Stanley Cup is all about."

CHAPTER 15

An Ode to Scarborough

2018 Washington Capitals
Devante Smith-Pelly

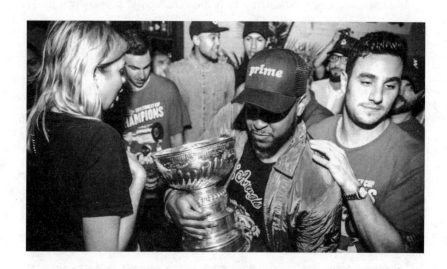

Scarborough is a suburb located on the east end of Toronto. Traditionally it's been an area of hardworking, blue-collar families. Scarborough is often treated as a punch line by people who live in the wealthier, elite neighborhoods of downtown Toronto.

"Scarberians," as they are sometimes called, couldn't care less. People who grew up in and live in Scarborough are proud of where they come from. Because there is one thing nobody can joke about it: the lengthy list of NHL players who grew up in Scarborough.

Rick Middleton, Larry Murphy, Rick Tocchet, Mike Ricci, Wayne Simmonds, Anson Carter, Kevin Weekes, brothers Anthony and Chris Stewart, Joel Ward, and Devante Smith-Pelly are all proud members of the Scarborough NHL family.

Smith-Pelly enjoyed playoff runs with Anaheim and Montreal during his career, but it wasn't until he joined the Washington Capitals that he would go all the way and become a Stanley Cup champion.

The Capitals, led by Alexander Ovechkin, had been building toward a championship for years. They won the Presidents' Trophy (for most game points in the season) two years in a row, in 2016 and 2017, and while they suffered playoff disappointments, they were always a threat. Entering the 2017–18 season, along with Ovechkin, the Capitals had a core of talented stars with Evgeny Kuznetsov, Nicklas Bäckström, and T. J. Oshie.

And they had grit. Smith-Pelly was known as a tough power forward, the kind of player who was hard on the forecheck and made teams pay for any mistakes. He was never one to back down from a fight either, and his teammates loved him for it. He wasn't called on to be a big goal scorer—in that season, he scored seven goals in seventy-five regular-season games.

But he came alive in the playoffs, scoring seven more, the biggest coming in the Cup Final against the Vegas Golden Knights: a game winner in game four, and the tying goal in game five. When the Capitals won game five to become Stanley Cup champions for the first time in the history of the franchise, Smith-Pelly's contributions couldn't be ignored. Every year, the NHL playoffs produce an unexpected hero, a player who has a nondescript regular season and then goes on to make a big impact in the postseason. In the 2018 Stanley Cup Final, Devante Smith-Pelly of Scarborough was that player. Vegas was prepared for everything, but they were not prepared for Smith-Pelly's unexpected goal scoring on the NHL's biggest stage.

A few years later, Brett Connolly told reporters, "He's probably the reason I have a [Stanley Cup] ring." That gives you an idea how much Smith-Pelly's heroics are regarded by his teammates. It was unexpected when long-suffering Capitals fans started chanting "D-S-P!" every time he scored in the postseason.

"I scored in the first game of the playoffs and there was a little D-S-P chant then. As playoffs moved on, it became a thing with the Capitals fans," said Smith-Pelly.

In the days following their victory, the Capitals players partied hard.

"We had a couple guys on that team who were partiers, but nobody could touch Ovechkin when it came to celebrating with the Cup after we won!" said Smith-Pelly.

After the victory parade through Washington, DC, there was a rally where Smith-Pelly held a classic wrestling title belt over his head as he stepped onto the stage. This was the same WWE title belt Smith-Pelly wore during the on-ice celebrations after the Capitals won it all, and the chants here were even louder.

And it was an honest-to-goodness custom title belt made by the WWE and wrestling superstar Triple H. The bejeweled WWE title belt has the Washington Capitals logo on the sides and a giant "WWE" on the front. To this day, Smith-Pelly doesn't know where it came from; it was just around, and he wore it.

"To hear the fans chant that at the parade and on the stage at the Cup rally, it was like an out-of-body experience," says Smith-Pelly. "I still think about going onstage that day and fans chanting like that. It is crazy to think about."

What is even crazier, in February, Smith-Pelly was the subject of racist taunts from unruly Blackhawks fans in Chicago. And sadly, it wasn't the first time that Smith-Pelly was forced to endure that kind of vile verbal garbage during his hockey career. Four months later, those same Blackhawks fans were forced to choke on their words as they watched a massive throng of Capitals fans chanting "D-S-P" during their Stanley Cup celebrations.

It was all a lot to process, but Smith-Pelly was already thinking about when he could take the Cup to his family and friends in Scarborough.

"Two or three weeks after we won, the Cup started making its rounds around the world. I got my day with the Cup in early August."

Smith-Pelly decided to make a stop on the way to Scarborough that was just as important to him as visiting home.

"I started my day by taking the Cup to Sick Kids Hospital in downtown Toronto," says Smith-Pelly. "A lot of the kids there are going through some tough things. I was there for close to three hours. I just wanted to do something to brighten their day as they go through some tough times. I wanted to walk through with the Cup and brighten up their day and see a couple of the kids smile. That was the whole idea behind my visit. I just wanted to do something nice for these kids. Then I went to the Black Dog Pub, near where I grew up in Scarborough, at Port Union and the 401. It's just around the corner from where my parents live and where I grew up. That was the first bar I ever went to because it was near my house. That is where guys like Wayne Simmonds lived, down the street from there. Our family used to go there for lunch, and my parents still go there all the time."

What Smith-Pelly could not have prepared for was the steady summer rain that was coming down at that point in the day. Despite the wet weather, people patiently waited a long time to hang out with Smith-Pelly and the Cup. Something that he still can't believe.

"It was crazy. I thought when the rain started it would be empty. But the line was still down the street! That meant a lot to me."

Devante Smith-Pelly is proud of his Scarborough roots, and he wanted to make sure the community was able to share in his success.

Among those who braved the rain to hang out with Smith-Pelly and the Stanley Cup was former NHLer and fellow Scarborough native Chris Stewart.

"I had an event there and I had some kids from minor hockey teams come through to see the Cup and people from the area stopped by as well," says Smith-Pelly. "After that, I had a private party for the adults. This was a night for my friends to hang out with me and the Cup. A lot of my friends are hockey fans, so for them to drink out of the Cup and touch and see it was cool. That entire day I spent with the Cup was an amazing experience.

"There had to be well over a hundred and fifty people at the private party downtown," Smith-Pelly continues. "It was all of my close friends, and anyone that I knew who I thought really wanted to come and stop by and see the Cup. We had a whole club rented out for the event. I drank a lot from the Cup that day, for sure! I didn't eat out of the Cup, but I drank a lot of beer and champagne out of the Cup that day. A couple of my friends did Jäger shots. One of my friends did a handstand shot out of the Cup. That was pretty funny."

Unlike most players who get to spend a day with the Stanley Cup, Smith-Pelly never had much alone time with it.

"Honestly, I never had any quiet time with the Cup. There was a little time in between hanging out at the Black Dog Pub and going downtown for the private party. I went home and relaxed for an hour. Other than that, I didn't really sit down and get a good look at the names on the Cup. The only time I did that was when we got our Stanley Cup rings. We had a team party, a ceremony, and that night I searched out my name on the Cup. I then took some time and looked at other names too. But when I had my day with the Cup, whenever it was around, it was basically party time."

Smith-Pelly is still humbled to be part of hockey history.

"Prior to game five of the Stanley Cup Final, Brooks Orpik, who had already won a Cup at the time, decided to say a few words. We were sitting in the dressing room with Brooks and young Jakub Vrana, who was twenty-one years old at the time. We were all talking about winning the Cup and Brooks started naming off guys who are Hall of Fame players and who are household names, and they have never won it. Brooks reminded us we had a chance to do something they never did and put our name on the Cup that night.

"Now that I think about it, Brooks was so right. You see guys in the NHL that having amazing careers and they play forever and score all these goals, and they never got their name on the Cup."

That understanding made Smith-Pelly determined to make the most of every second that he had the Cup.

"When I knew that I was going to get my day with the Cup, I tried to plan it out to not waste a second of my time. Even after I felt like I had a pretty busy day—and a lot of people saw the Cup and a lot of people got a chance to take a picture with it—at the end of the day, at midnight, I wanted more. I said to myself at the end, 'Oh man, I wish I had the Cup a little bit longer.' It was an action-packed day, but I am glad that I did what I did, and I stopped where I stopped. I made sure a lot of people who normally would not have been able to see the Cup got to see it that day."

Smith-Pelly has many photos that he cherishes from that championship. One of them is of him holding the Stanley Cup while standing beside an ice sculpture of him holding the Cup after the Capitals won. That ice sculpture was made possible by one of his teammates.

"Brett Connolly's wife somehow found that. It was a great addition to the celebration."

But there is one photo that will always stand out above the rest.

"It is me and my grandparents and the Stanley Cup. Everything about that day was special, but that moment was incredibly special."

The entire experience imprinted itself on Smith-Pelly forever. "From going to Sick Kids Hospital, right until the end, the amount of people that got to experience the Cup was important to me. Living in the Toronto area, this is a pretty big hockey town. To see everyone get so excited when they saw the Cup was great. Then to see everyone get even more excited to help me celebrate that day was even better."

Smith-Pelly knew how fortunate he was—how rare a thing it is to win it all—and made sure his day with the Stanley Cup was all about family, friends, and the community where he grew up.

"I loved spending time with my friends and my parents and my grandparents that day," says Smith-Pelly. "I loved watching my grandparents lift the Stanley Cup over their head. Stuff like that means a lot to me. We have a close family, so we would spend a lot of time together. I am pretty sure my grandparents became hockey fans when they lived in Fort McMurray during the heyday of Wayne Gretzky and the Edmonton Oilers. It was cool seeing my grandparents get to touch the Cup. It was cool seeing my friends and how excited they were. Obviously, they are incredibly supportive, but to see how excited they actually were when they got a chance to drink out of the Cup really sticks with me. Our grandparents were always there for us. No matter what, our family could always count on my grandparents. I couldn't think of a better way to thank them for all their years of love and devotion to our family than to let them lift the Stanley Cup over their heads. Nobody can ever take that moment away from me, and I will cherish it forever.

"Getting a chance for my family and friends to celebrate with me on achieving something that they knew I wanted to do since I was five years old, it was a good day."

A good day for Scarborough, and a very good day for Devante Smith-Pelly and his family and friends.

CHAPTER 16

Ice Cream Tastes Better from the Stanley Cup

2019 St. Louis Blues
Robert Thomas

Located thirty minutes north of Toronto, Aurora is a classic Canadian bedroom community. Away from the bright lights of the big city, Aurora is a good place to raise a family. It is home to Magna auto parts, St. Andrew's College, and some excellent hockey players. Robert Thomas of the St. Louis Blues is a perfect example of that. Thomas was raised in

Aurora and played his minor hockey there before moving to London, Ontario, to play in the OHL.

The year before making the Blues, Thomas was traded from the London Knights to the Hamilton Bulldogs. Thomas helped lead the Bulldogs to an OHL championship and they made it to the semifinals of the Memorial Cup. In October, Thomas made the St. Louis Blues out of training camp. His first season in the NHL was an eventful one. His first coach, Mike Yeo, was fired in November and replaced by Craig Berube. The Blues started the 2019 calendar year with the worst record in the NHL, 15–18–4. In one of the great in-season turnarounds in recent memory, the Blues went on a run. By March 29, the same team that was dead last January 1 had clinched a spot in the postseason. They beat the Winnipeg Jets in six games and needed seven games to beat the Stars, and they needed six games to beat the Sharks and advance. In the Cup Final, the Blues needed all seven games to beat the Boston Bruins and win the Cup for the first time in the history of the franchise.

"We had a large group of guys who had been in the playoffs before, and we had quality veterans. I came in as a nineteen-year-old and I was trying to take it all in as I competed in the NHL playoffs for the first time. Just being in the playoffs was cool, everything after that was gravy," said Thomas.

If just being in the playoffs was gravy, then the main course took place May 7, 2019, when Thomas set up Pat Maroon in double overtime to eliminate the Dallas Stars and advance to the Western Conference Final.

"That was a face-off play that we had run a bunch of times," says Thomas. "Tyler Bozak is a great face-off guy, and he wins a lot of face-offs on his strong side. Prior to the face-off, Bozak and Pat Maroon looked at me and gave me the nod. I knew the play was coming. Earlier in the series we tried to run it on John Klingberg, and he stuffed me right away along the wall. On this night, I saw him standing over there, so I knew I had to make a move to get by him. I was lucky enough to squeak through on the inside and get a shot off. Maroon grabbed the rebound, scored, and we won the series."

However, by the time the Blues met the Bruins in the Stanley Cup Final, Thomas was battling a nasty injury on the wrist he'd previously had surgery on.

"I hurt my wrist in the Dallas series in the second round and I was fighting tooth and nail to get into the lineup every night. Unfortunately, I was only able to dress for two games in the Cup Finals against the Bruins," says Thomas.

Even though he wasn't in the lineup that night, Thomas was a big part of the celebrations on June 12 when the Blues beat the Bruins to become Stanley Cup champions for the first time.

"Winning the Cup and that night . . . it took a while for it all to sink in. Even throughout the playoffs, I would talk to other players on the team that I was close friends with. They had been in the league for a while and they would tell me, 'This isn't normal. You are so young; you really have to take advantage of this.'

"And they were so right," Thomas continues. "I was just a kid who had a lot of success in minor hockey and in junior and I played on some good teams. With the Blues in the 2019 playoffs, I just kept going for it and I got lucky. It was a cool experience, that's for sure. In the moment, being on the ice, and raising the Stanley Cup over my head, I didn't realize what I had just accomplished at the time. A couple of years later, I look back on that night and it amazes me. Watching Tampa win and Colorado win in the years after us, I can see the seconds ticking off and they are about to win, that is when I think about that night winning the Cup. It really sinks in at that moment and it is something that I am enormously proud about."

The night was made even better for the presence of his family.

"I had my whole family in Boston that night for game seven. They were on the ice with me, helping me celebrate. It is a moment we will have forever."

Thomas was nearly overwhelmed by the reaction from the fans in St. Louis after they won.

"The reaction from the city of St. Louis after we won was out of this world. Even if we are fortunate enough to win another, I don't think anything will top the reaction from the city from that first one," relates Thomas. "The parade through the city was so exciting. No matter where you were in the city over the next few weeks after we won, people were celebrating. I would be walking down the street to get groceries, and people would honk their horn and wave. It felt like the whole city shut down for the next few weeks after we won."

Before the parties had a chance to die down, the planning was already well under way for the Cup tour that summer. When he was asked where he was going to spend a day with the Cup, he immediately knew the answer: it was coming to his hometown of Aurora.

"A few weeks after we won, the Hockey Hall of Fame were busy setting up the schedule for the Cup tour that summer. We have a lot of Toronto-area guys on the team, so they had a lot of planning to do. They gave us the date and then the real planning began."

Thomas turned twenty on July 2, and on July 29 it was his day with the Cup, a day he took very seriously.

"I spent a lot of time with my family planning the day and how we could get the community involved. We wanted to involve the York-Simcoe Express, St. Andrew's College, and all those things that meant a lot to me becoming a Stanley Cup champion. That was a big part of what we wanted to do with our day with the Cup. We wanted to celebrate and show our thanks to Aurora and all these organizations for what they did for me."

Thanks to an overworked Keeper of the Cup, Thomas got the Cup earlier than he expected.

"Mike Bolt, one of the Keepers of the Cup, texted me the night before my day and said, Hey, we can get the Cup to you an hour early if me and my partner can have a hot shower. I laughed. That was probably the easiest request I ever said yes to!

"Mike Bolt and his associate showed up with the Cup over an hour before I thought it was going to be there. It was around seven thirty in the morning when they showed up. It was nice and I had the whole family at my parents' house. Before everything took place and it got too busy, we were able to grab a ton of photos with the Cup."

Thomas admits that he had a near-out-of-body experience as he looked at all the names on the Cup.

"I looked at names like Sidney Crosby and others on the Cup. I had to pinch myself to realize that my name is on the same trophy as guys like him. I ran through the names, and I could see so many great players that I watched growing up. I come from a big hockey family and all of our friends are big hockey fans. They loved going through all the names of players they watched. It was one of those moments you see the emotion of everyone as they spent time looking at the Cup."

Not long afterwards, Thomas and his family embarked on a whirl-wind day to make sure as many people in Aurora as possible got a chance to see the Stanley Cup.

"After spending time with the Cup at home, we went to St. Andrew's College. I went to high school there and I took the Cup to some of the kids' summer camps they have there. I showed the Cup to a number of my favorite teachers and staff members, and I got my photo with them. I just wanted to show my appreciation for all of the stuff they had done for me over the years. From there, we went into the Aurora Community Centre arena. I took some photos there with the York-Simcoe Express teams. Playing minor hockey with the Express was a huge part of where I am today. I took photos with all the teams from novice to minor midget. I played for the York-Simcoe

Express organization for eight years. We won the OMHA champion-ship when I was in bantam, and I still remember that.

"From there, we took the Cup to Machell Park for a rally," Thomas continues. "Mayor Tom Mrakas and the town of Aurora did a fantastic job setting everything up. My family really loved it. We are proud to be from Aurora and there was a good turnout to see me and the Cup. I was able to see a lot of family and friends and even some people that I'd lost touch with over the years."

As Thomas weaved his way through the crowd to bring the Cup onto a stage at Machell Park for a rally put on by the town, a young kid reached out and touched the Cup, a moment that was not lost on Thomas.

"I know when I was seven or eight years old, I would have loved to be able to see the Stanley Cup and to touch it," says Thomas. "Those are the moments that really touch you. To be able to give a young kid an experience like that, that felt great. I know it is something I would have loved at his age. I was happy I was able to give him that. Certain moments like that stand out, but generally the day was a blur of activity and excitement. The day moves along so quickly. I didn't really understand what just happened until a couple days afterwards. We had a photographer taking pictures throughout the day. He took so many great photos of everything that happened. A week later we received the photo book, and as we looked at all of the pictures, that is when it really hit me—I actually did it, I was a Stanley Cup champion."

There were more stops throughout Aurora before the day was over. And for anyone who lives there, getting some ice cream at Dairy Queen on Yonge Street is a real treat. And Robert Thomas was no different.

"After the park, we stopped at McAlpine Ford. They have been good to our family over the years, and they provided the cars for our day with the Cup. I am a big ice cream lover, so after McAlpine Ford, I took the Cup to Dairy Queen. I got them to make a Blizzard in the

Cup. A bunch of kids were there when I arrived, and we all ate ice cream from the Cup. From there, we headed back to the house for a night with family and friends and a backyard party."

Most players drink beer out of the Stanley Cup, but the Thomas family did things a little differently.

"We made a big Moscow Mule in the Cup. My mom loves that drink, and so does my girlfriend. I enjoy them too."

Not only did Thomas drink from the Cup, but he also ate some of his mom's cooking out of it as well.

"My mom makes these chocolate chip cookies. At Christmastime, she makes at least thirty dozen cookies. That is what we give our family and friends as presents. She made a ton of cookies, and we filled up the Cup so everyone could have one."

When he wasn't drinking Moscow Mules and eating chocolate chip cookies out of the Cup, he was sharing it with as many people as possible.

"I have so many people that meant so much to me over the years. My billet family from London, the Owens, came down to visit. They helped me a lot in junior hockey, and I was happy to share the Cup with them. My billets in Hamilton, the Sordos, they came, and they are amazing. Those two families coming to Aurora to see me was awesome.

"I loved having all of my cousins and grandparents and my aunts and uncles with me that day," says Thomas. "A lot of my family were able to get to a bunch of my games in the playoffs. The biggest thing for me that day was observing people's reaction when they saw the Cup. Some people cried and some people were so happy to finally lift the Stanley Cup. Of course, the rule is that I also must be holding the Stanley Cup at the same time. They don't like people lifting the Cup without the player also holding on at the same time. Seeing all of that emotion, that was special."

All good things come to an end, and soon Thomas's day was done.

"Mike Bolt left with the Cup very early the next morning. He left Aurora to go to Buttonville Airport and take a private plane to Quebec to take the Cup to David Perron. He and the Cup left around twelve thirty in the morning, and we were still up, enjoying our time with it. As much as I wanted to spend more time with the Cup, I understand how hard it is for the Keepers of the Cup. Especially with all of the travel that they have throughout the summer. They are the best and they take good care of you all day. No matter what the challenge, they find a way through it and make it all work."

It wasn't long after the euphoria of being a Stanley Cup champion died down that Thomas wanted to get back to work so he could win it again.

"After winning the Stanley Cup my first year in the NHL, my attitude was, 'Oh, we can win it every year.' The year after, we watched Tampa win the Cup and I hated it. I told myself, 'Once we lose in the playoffs, I am never watching another game that season!' That feeling of winning the Stanley Cup definitely motivates me every summer. Trust me, winning the Cup is a lot more fun than losing!"

Aurora has evolved quite a bit over the years, but it still has a small-town feel. And to Thomas, that is a good thing.

"I love Aurora and I love living here. I love coming home every summer and being with my family. That's why I wanted to share the Cup with as many people in Aurora as possible, with so many people that mean everything to me."

The motto of Aurora, which you see on signs as you enter town, is "You're in good company." Robert Thomas showed everyone from the mayor on down what that really means.

CHAPTER 17

Worth the Wait

2021 Tampa Bay Lightning
Jon Cooper

In the lengthy list of Stanley Cup–winning coaches, few, if any, had a path to success as unusual as Jon Cooper of the Tampa Bay Lightning.

Cooper is a perfect example of the saying "It doesn't matter where you start, it matters where you end up." And in 2020 and 2021, Jon Cooper ended up on the top of the mountain as his Tampa Bay Lightning became back-to-back Stanley Cup champions.

Once upon a time, Cooper played hockey for the Notre Dame Hounds in Wilcox, Saskatchewan. Notre Dame produced NHL stars like Wendel Clark, Curtis Joseph, Vincent Lecavalier, and Brad Richards. That is about as far as Cooper's competitive hockey career took him. After going to school at Hofstra University on Long Island, New York, Cooper went to law school in Michigan. By the time he was in his early thirties, Jon Cooper was a public defender and playing beer league hockey for a team called the Legal Eagles.

One of the members of that team was a local judge. That judge's son needed a coach for his high school hockey team. And with that, the coaching career of Jon Cooper began.

Cooper started at the bottom of the coaching ladder and more than paid his dues along the way. Cooper learned the skill of getting his message across to his players. He both taught and motivated them to get the most out of them every game. Cooper also made it a mission to never stop learning about hockey, including his players and what made them tick. He never acted like he knew it all, and he was constantly finding ways to coach better, lead better, motivate better, and communicate better with his players. While Cooper quietly went out about his business, he won championships at every level he coached.

In the 1999–2000 season, he coached the Lansing Catholic High School team to their first state championship in twenty-five years. From there Cooper coached the Metro Stars to the USA Junior B championship. Cooper went on to coach the HoneyBaked midget major AAA team out of Detroit. His coaching journey led him to Texarkana, Texas, where part of his duties included chasing rats from the rink and helping to put up the boards and glass for game day. The franchise moved to St. Louis, and he led them to the NAHL championship. He moved to Green Bay, Wisconsin, and won a championship in the USHL. Two years later, he led the AHL's Norfolk Admirals to a Calder Cup championship. Cooper and his family were constantly on the move, and they were winning at every stop along the way.

The next year, Cooper was coaching the Syracuse Crunch, the AHL farm team of the Tampa Bay Lightning. In March 2013, Cooper was named the new head coach of the Lightning. After winning the Cup in 2004, the team had gone into a decline and there'd been some big changes. Steve Yzerman became the new GM in 2010 and started to make waves. Cooper inherited a team with a strong core of players, including Steven Stamkos, Victor Hedman, and Nikita Kucherov. The club quickly turned a corner and became a real Cup contender. In 2015, the Lightning got all the way to the Cup Final but lost to the Chicago Blackhawks. In 2019 the Lightning were the Presidents' Trophy winners and the number one seed in the NHL playoffs, but, shockingly, were then swept in the first round by the Columbus Blue Jackets.

The following season was one for the history books. With Covid-19 canceling part of the season, the playoffs took place in two "bubble" cities—Toronto in the east and Edmonton in the west—where teams could stay together safely. The team again advanced to the final, this time facing the Dallas Stars, an underdog team that had fought their way through the Western Conference. But they were no match for Jon Cooper and the Lightning.

The bubble experience robbed the Lightning of playing and winning in front of their fans. In fact, there were no fans in the stands for any team, due to Covid-19 restrictions. Still, as the seconds ticked down and the Lightning won, Jon Cooper, a man who started at the bottom and overcame the odds, was flooded with emotions.

"It is hard to say the exact emotion. It is a fine line between exhilaration and relief," he says. "I would be hard-pressed not to say that relief was my biggest emotion when we won in 2020. For so long, you are chasing something. With every year that goes by that you don't win, the feeling that you want to win keeps getting bigger. To a point that it keeps people in hockey. There are some longtime, veteran players in the NHL, if they had won the Cup early in their career, I don't know if they would have played as long as they have. Maybe they would have, but for guys in the NHL, there is that ultimate chase of trying to win the Stanley Cup. When you win it, there's a flood of emotions that come out of you, and the biggest one is relief. And there is also a little bit of disbelief."

Despite his late start as a coach, Cooper's desire to constantly learn and improve and win paid off. Cooper won championships at every level he coached at. And eventually, he won the biggest prize in the biggest league of them all, the coveted Stanley Cup.

Playing in the bubble, away from family and friends, was hard enough, but winning during the pandemic meant that nobody got to spend a day with the Cup that summer.

"When we won in 2020, we were told that the Stanley Cup wasn't leaving the country. That automatically shut down my plans of taking the Cup to my family in Canada. It hit me, *Wow, we win the Stanley Cup, we realized our ultimate dream, and we can't share it.*

But nothing could ruin the bond that Cooper formed with his players. "When you win a Stanley Cup, the guys go from being players that you coach to becoming family members."

Cooper and his new extended family were still coming to grips with the fact that they were not going to be able to enjoy something they had been pursuing for so long.

"The biggest part of winning the Cup is sharing it. In some ways, sharing the Cup with others is almost better than raising it above your head on the ice. Sharing the Cup with people and seeing their reactions is an amazing feeling. When you are not afforded the ability to share it with others, that was discouraging."

Because of the ongoing Covid crisis, the next season wouldn't begin until January 13, 2021. In this shortened season, the playoffs got under way on May 15 and the Lightning were on a mission. They wanted to win a Stanley Cup in front of their hometown fans. Despite injuries and some tough competition, the team flew through the playoffs with that singular goal in mind. Finally, on July 7, before a packed house at Amalie Arena in Tampa Bay, the Lightning defeated the Montreal Canadiens 1–0, closing the series to repeat as Stanley Cup champions.

"I find it completely ironic that we won the Stanley Cup the next year on home ice in Tampa," says Cooper. "For us to do that, with basically the exact same team as we had the year before, I thought was our way of giving Covid a slap in the face and saying, 'No, you didn't win.' We won again, and we were able to celebrate the right way."

Cooper and the Lightning were determined to make up for what happened the year before.

Jon Cooper with the Great One

"In the end, the players all got their day with the Cup. A few players that were not with us the next year, like Kevin Shattenkirk, he got his day with the Cup. Even though he was on another team by then, we made sure nobody missed out on having their day."

For years, Jon Cooper and his family have spent the summer in Coeur d'Alene, Idaho.

"Coeur d'Alene is a little piece of happiness to me. The weather is beautiful, there is a golf course, there is a lake, there's mountains, with zero humidity and no bugs! It checks a lot of summertime boxes for me. It really fits for what I am looking for in the offseason."

Cooper was determined to make sure that Coeur d'Alene had an experience with the Stanley Cup that the town would never forget.

"The sense of pride that I had my day with the Cup was overwhelming. I was determined to let everyone in town be a part of my day. In the summer of 2021, they said that the coach, the GM, and the captain would all get the Cup for two days. Tyler Johnson lives pretty close to my summer home, so, after I had the Cup for two days, he got it the next day."

Cooper ended up sharing the Cup that day with a friend of his, a friend who has won the Stanley Cup four times.

"The power of the Stanley Cup is something that you have to see to believe. I have been truly fortunate in my life, and I have become friends with Wayne Gretzky. Every time that you are with Wayne, he is the trophy in the room. The only time that I saw that Wayne wasn't the 'trophy' was when the Stanley Cup was in the room. And when the Cup was in the room, Wayne became a kid, just like the rest of us. It was remarkable to watch Wayne Gretzky turn into a twelve-year-old, chasing his dream, and here was a guy that won it four times."

Like Gretzky, Cooper had dreamed about spending a day with the Cup for a long time.

"When I was growing up, every time someone would ask me about what my goals were, my goal was to have my name on the Stanley Cup. As I got older, it was obvious I wasn't going to make it as a player. It was still in the back of my mind that somehow, I might be an executive on a team that wins the Cup. I never thought I would be a coach of a team that won the Cup. Later on, I found my passion and found something I was good at. And when those two things came together, I knew what I was meant to do in life, and that was coaching."

Throughout the day, Cooper kept looking at the Cup, and the magnitude of his achievement was overwhelming.

"When I looked at the Cup, I knew for at least the next sixty years, my kids, my grandkids, could all look at the Stanley Cup and say, 'My dad, my grandfather, is on there.' By winning the Cup and having my name on it, I was putting my stamp on hockey history. That was a cool thing for me when I realized that."

Jon Cooper also realized the Stanley Cup's mystical powers as he and a group of friends stopped at a local watering hole for a drink.

"I had a big day planned. I had all these boxes on my list I wanted to check. I took it to the kids at the Wayne Gretzky hockey school. I took it to the local sheriff's department and shared it with the first responders. Then I was going to have a golf event. The same day we did the golf event, I took the Stanley Cup to a couple of establishments in town. One of them is considered one of the oldest dive bars in the state of Idaho. It is a grungy old place that has a ton of charm. About the last thing you expect in this place is the Stanley Cup. I had at least fifteen people with me in one of those extended vans. We walked into the bar, and there were only six people there. They looked like people that had been at the bar for a while and they looked like longtime regulars. I plopped the Stanley Cup down and my friends gathered around the bar to get a drink. This gentleman that was there, he was at least in his late seventies. He looked at me and said, 'Is that the Stanley Cup?' I said, yes, it is. 'Is that Wayne Gretzky?' I said, yes, it is. 'Is that John Elway?' I said, yes, it is. (He was in town for a charity golf tournament.) He looked at me and said, 'If I walked outside right now and got hit by a bus, I would die a happy man. I never thought in my life I would ever be a part of this. This is the coolest day of my life.' He sat down, lit up a cigarette, ordered himself a beer, and never said another word. That was my 'wow' moment of the power of the Stanley Cup."

Like anyone else in the world, Jon Cooper has some down days. But there are two photos from his day with the Cup that bring him instant happiness.

"There is one photo in Idaho that I love—it is my three kids eating Lucky Charms out of the Stanley Cup. And during the final party we held before the Cup was leaving, somebody took a picture of me pouring beer into my wife's mouth with the Stanley Cup. This is one of my all-time favorite photos."

As far as what Cooper had to drink out of the Cup, it was nothing unusual. "I drank beer and champagne and a little Crown Royal rye whisky. Just as an ode to my Canadian roots."

However, drinking out of the Cup led to Cooper suffering an unexpected injury.

"Yes, you get to drink out of the Stanley Cup. And there are all these unwritten rules about the Cup. If you never won the Cup, you are not allowed to raise it over your head. You can touch it, but unless you won the Cup, you can't do anything with it. Since I won the Cup, I was the person that poured whatever drink was inside it into the mouth of somebody else. I had the Cup for two days, then we had this big party at the end of my time. There must have been close to one thousand people at this party. I basically stood on a bar for hours on end, holding the Stanley Cup, and everyone lined up to drink out of it. The next day, I woke up and said, 'Oh my God. I think I got arthritis.' I could barely move my fingers and my forearm! That is the sacrifice you have to make when you have your day with the Cup. I was almost on the NHL's injured reserve list for twenty-four hours because I poured so much beer for so long out of the Cup, I had sore fingers!"

Cooper admits that it is a bittersweet feeling when the Cup leaves.

"It is a sense of relief when you win the Stanley Cup and sometimes there is a tiny bit of relief when the Keeper of the Cup comes and takes it away. Those two days . . . I don't know if planning a wedding was harder. It was a forty-eight-hour nonstop celebration."

You would think that because he had the Cup for two days, he would have got some quality alone time with the trophy. That didn't happen for Cooper.

"During those forty-eight hours, I had the Cup by myself for exactly one hour. And that was when I was asked to do a socially distanced, sit-down interview with the Stanley Cup. [The reporter was far apart from him.] I cherished that time. Nobody was in the house, and I was sitting on our back deck. I was overlooking the golf course and it was just me and the Stanley Cup."

Little did Cooper know that his quiet time with the Cup would be interrupted by a golf foursome that featured three Hall of Fame athletes.

"So, I am sitting there with the Stanley Cup on my back deck, and I live on one of the holes of this golf course. These four guys were playing, and they started walking over because they spotted the Stanley Cup. They come over and say, 'Is that the Stanley Cup?' I said yes, it is, come on over. Then it dawned on me, holy shit! There was a celebrity charity golf tournament going on at the same time I had the Cup. The four guys that walked over to me were Richard Dent, Ozzie Smith, Vince Coleman, and Marcus Allen! I could not believe it. I have a picture with me holding the Cup and hanging out with those four guys. They just happened to be playing that hole while I was sitting by myself, smoking a cigar, and hanging with the Cup."

Winning the Stanley Cup brings fame and fortune, but all the fame and money in the world could not equal what Cooper's wife, Jessie, means to him.

"The big thing for me in my life is my wife. My kids look up to me.

They are growing up and their only memories are of our time in Tampa. Even though my son was born in Green Bay and my girls were born in St. Louis, those were just stops on the road, and they don't even remember those cities. Most of their life has been spent in Tampa. But Jessie, my wife, we met when I got into coaching. When I left my law practice in Michigan in 1999 and went to Texarkana, Texas, to coach, she was just graduating law school. She threw caution to the wind and said, 'I'm coming with you.' She spent three years with me in Texarkana, then two years in St. Louis, then two in Green Bay, two years in Norfolk, one year in Syracuse, and finally in Tampa. Everyone talks to me about putting up the boards and glass in Texarkana, and I was, but so was Jessie. She sacrificed her law career for something that we never dreamt would end up the way it did.

"I wasn't coaching for money; the end goal wasn't 'I'm going to end up in the NHL and make big money.' None of that matters at all. As long as you have enough money to put food on the table, you are good. That is why coaching was the perfect job for me. When I started coaching, I never looked at a clock again the rest my life."

When Cooper took the Stanley Cup to the Wayne Gretzky hockey school, he spoke to the kids about the message that you should "take nothing for granted" in life. It was an important message for the kids to hear, and it is a motto that Cooper lives by every day.

"People feel I am more relatable than other coaches in the NHL, because a lot of coaches played in the NHL. Other people with a passion and knowledge of hockey might want to follow in my footsteps and try to become an NHL coach someday. I had a different background. There are times they say, 'I want to do what you did.' I tell them, I know you do, and you *can* do what I did. You have to understand there is a gap between me standing here with the Stanley Cup and when you first start out. That is why I feel it is so important to not forget where you came from and keep your humility. And you have to believe in yourself. Bet on yourself and be humble, work hard, and be good to people. Then see what happens."

True to his word, Jon Cooper bet on himself. He is humble to a fault, he works extremely hard, and he is incredibly good to people. And he gave Coeur d'Alene, Idaho, a Stanley Cup experience they will never forget.

CHAPTER 18

A Cup Full of Pierogies

2022 Colorado Avalanche
Darcy Kuemper

Darcy Kuemper with his grandparents

Days after Darcy Kuemper helped the Colorado Avalanche beat the Tampa Bay Lightning to win the Stanley Cup in 2022, he started the countdown until he could take the Cup to his hometown of Saskatoon.

Hockey in Saskatchewan is as quintessentially Canadian as maple syrup, Terry Fox, the beaver, and inukshuks. The same province that produced Gordie Howe, Wendel Clark, Bryan Trottier, and Johnny Bower also produced a championship goalie who is deeply proud of his Saskatchewan roots.

Darcy Kuemper is also a classic example of a late bloomer. He didn't start playing in the WHL until he was eighteen years old. Kuemper was a sixth-round draft pick, 161st overall by the Minnesota Wild in the 2009 NHL entry draft. It would take thirteen years from the day he was drafted until the day he lifted the Stanley Cup over his head.

As a wise man once said, "It is the journey, not the destination," and Kuemper tried to make the most of every step along the way in his journey to becoming a Stanley Cup champion.

After stops with the Minnesota Wild, the Los Angeles Kings, and the Arizona Coyotes, Kuemper was traded to the Colorado Avalanche in July 2021. From the second he arrived he knew there was something special about this Avalanche team. "The very first time I spoke to anyone in the organization, they all said the same thing: 'We are going to win the Cup this year.'"

That confidence continued throughout the season. "Honestly, going into the playoffs, we were considered the favorites to win it all," says Kuemper. "For most of the season, our attitude was 'Stanley Cup or bust,' which is different than some other teams. From the first game of the playoffs, our attitude in the dressing room was that we are going to win the Cup. It is going to happen. We had that mindset all the way through the playoffs."

After a shaky outing in game three of the Stanley Cup Final, Kuemper bounced back with an impressive performance in game four. In fact, Kuemper made history that night, becoming the first goalie ever to have an assist on an overtime goal in a Stanley Cup Final game.

"I don't know if my performance in game four was the best of my career. But with everything going on and getting over the mental hurdle of having a bad game in game three, to be able to bounce back game four is what I am most proud of."

When the Avs were trying to close out the series in game six, Kuemper watched helplessly as Gabriel Landeskog lost a skate blade a few feet in front of him. "It was a two-to-one game late in the third period, and the Lightning were pushing hard to tie the game. We were doing everything we could to defend the lead. Tampa has a shot on goal and Landeskog sticks out his leg and makes an incredible shot block, and the blade of his skate falls out. At that point, they have a two-man advantage and Landeskog is crawling around, trying to get off the ice. We got the puck out of our end, and I yelled, 'Quick, someone get him off the ice before they come back!' That's when Nathan MacKinnon dragged him off the ice."

After the Avalanche won it all and commissioner Gary Bettman handed the team the Stanley Cup, Kuemper patiently waited for his turn to do something he had dreamed about his whole life.

"When it was my turn to skate around with the Cup, a lot of things were going through my mind. Being the fact that I was a late bloomer and that I had been around the NHL for a while, I realized what an accomplishment it was to win the Stanley Cup. It hit me how fortunate I was to be on the right team and in the right situation to win it all. The amount of appreciation that I felt in that moment was almost overwhelming. I skated around with the Cup over my head and looking back on my career. Even better, my family was there, and they had done so much for me over the years to even get to that point. I was so emotional; I was joyful and thankful for everybody that had helped me get to that point."

After that, it was time for a time-honored tradition that started with Wayne Gretzky and the 1988 Edmonton Oilers, the coveted team photo on the ice with the Stanley Cup. Kuemper still gets chills looking at it.

"That photo is something that all of us that participated in winning that Stanley Cup will hang on to for the rest of our lives. In the moment itself, that is the first time the entire team gathers around the Stanley Cup. We were able to soak in the moment of what we had just accomplished as they took the photo. To win a Stanley Cup, everyone on the team needs to play a crucial role. To me, we don't win the Cup without contributions from everyone in that photo."

As happy as Darcy Kuemper was for himself, he was just as happy for his older teammates who had been waiting a long time to lift the Stanley Cup over their head.

"It was great to see Andrew Cogliano win a Cup. It was great to see a guy like Erik Johnson win. He had been with the Avalanche organization forever and he was there during some really tough times. Erik was with the Avs when they were at the bottom of the league, so to see him win was remarkable, really. He stuck with the Avs and played a vital role in the team getting back to the top."

Soon after the parades and the parties ended, players and coaches submitted their requests to have a day with the Stanley Cup. Kuemper freely admits that his wife was the driving force behind organizing their special day.

"In early July we found out we were getting the Cup in early August. My wife, Sydney, helped a lot planning the day. It was almost like planning a wedding. We were trying to organize one big day. We wanted to find a nice balance where we gave back to the community a little bit. But also, we wanted to enjoy the Stanley Cup with our family and friends. My mindset for that day was, what was the best way to share the Cup with the people that helped me get there? Thanks to my wife, the day went great, and it was so much fun."

Kuemper admits to acting like a kid on Christmas morning, waiting for the Stanley Cup to arrive. "The Keeper of the Cup arrived around ten in the morning. I remember waking up and I kept checking my phone to see if he was going to text me that he was going to be there early."

That day started soon after the Cup arrived when Kuemper took the Stanley Cup to Jim Pattison Children's Hospital in Saskatoon. "I remember before the children's hospital was even in Saskatoon, a lot of the local hockey players would help out and volunteer, as the community was trying to raise money to build the hospital. I felt a connection to the hospital, and it was something that was important to my wife and me. We don't know what the kids and the families are going through, but we knew how difficult it must be for those families. To be able to share the Cup with them, and to be able to share some joy with them, that was especially important to us."

From there, Darcy Kuemper took the Stanley Cup to somewhere else that is also important to him. Kuemper's father is a veteran sergeant with the Saskatoon Police Service and taking the Cup to their headquarters was a real highlight. "I always looked up to my dad growing up my whole life. The two things I wanted to be growing up whenever anyone would ask me, I wanted to play in the NHL, or I wanted to be a police officer. To bring the Cup to my dad's workplace was a proud moment for me. I know it was also a proud moment for him as well, to be able to share the Stanley Cup with his coworkers at the Saskatoon police services. I wanted to show my appreciation for what all the police officers do for us on a daily basis. It is what my dad has done his whole career."

When Darcy had precious quiet time with the Stanley Cup, he did what all players do: he started looking at names of past champions. "I had a lot of fun looking at the Cup and looking back at the different teams. What stood out the most to me was all of the dynasty teams on the Cup. There are a number of teams that won the Cup multiple times, and you would see certain names repeated numerous times. I broke into the NHL in February of 2013, and I remember playing against guys that I grew up watching. I played against guys that were heroes of mine growing up, and looking at the Cup, I could see their names."

Darcy ate only one thing out of the Cup that day, and it was a longtime Saskatchewan favorite. "I did eat some pierogies out of the Stanley Cup, with bacon and sour cream. A classic Saskatchewan dish. However, I put a bowl inside of the bowl of the Cup to help keep it clean. The Keeper of the Cup was very appreciative of that."

Darcy Kuemper is a family-first kind of person, and he was on a mission to share the Cup with every generation of his family. "My grandparents are getting older, and it is getting tough for them to come to big events. My grandparents came over to my parents' house before we went to the evening party. My wife and I spent an hour with them and with my aunts and uncles. Just to be able to share the Stanley Cup with them was one of my favorite moments from that day."

Not long after his grandparents and aunts and uncles left, Kuemper took the Stanley Cup to a large party with family and friends. "That was a fun way to wrap up the day, enjoying the Stanley Cup with my

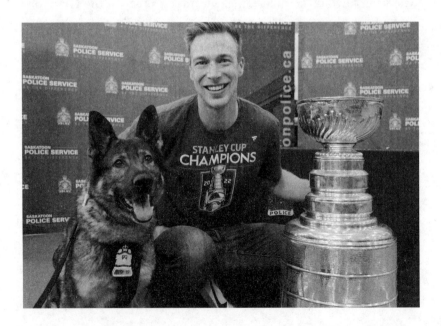

friends and family. It was bit of a party with everyone, and I was able to share the Cup with so many people that I wasn't able to throughout the day. These were friends that I grew up playing hockey with and we went to school with. They were there and their parents were there as well. They were the parents that would carpool me and my friends to practices and games. It was so much fun.

"We drank more than a few beers out of the Stanley Cup that night," Kuemper continues. "We had a steady lineup of people, waiting for their turn to drink out of the Cup. Everyone enjoyed themselves."

Darcy Kuemper learned the hard way that the Stanley Cup summer tour is run on a very tight schedule. "The Keeper took the Cup away at twelve sharp, right at midnight. He was giving me the half-an-hour countdown, the fifteen-minute countdown, the ten-minute countdown. Then he told me five minutes left, only one minute left, and then he packed the Stanley Cup in the protective road case, and he left. It was gone, right at twelve."

Like all players, Kuemper's day with the Cup went way too fast. "When the Keeper took the Cup, it all kind of snuck up on me. Even though he kept warning me about the time, for some reason, I was thinking in the back of my mind that I was going to get some extra time with the Cup. He looked at me and said, 'No, Darcy, it has to go.' It all happened pretty quickly. It was sad to see it go because that entire day was the highlight of such an incredible summer. The next day, it was back to work and time to start preparing for the next season."

When the next day arrived, Darcy was back to his normal offseason daily routine. Later on, the enormity of having his name etched into the Stanley Cup really hit him. "It is so special to think that my name is on the Stanley Cup. By next season, I was busy playing and wouldn't think about it too much. Then I might be on social media and see photos of us winning the Cup. Or a friend would send me a photo of the two of us with the Cup. It would instantly bring a smile to my face. And I am sure every time that I see the Cup, it will bring a smile to my face for the rest of my life."

Now that he has his name on the Stanley Cup, Kuemper is determined to do everything possible to win it again and spend another day with his friends and family in Saskatoon.

"There are so many special days after you win the Stanley Cup. From the day that you win it, to the first day you are back in the city with your teammates, to the day of the parade and the day you bring the Cup to your hometown. These are some of the best days of your life. After you do it, I kept thinking, *Wow, I would love to do that again.* It crosses my mind often and it pushes me to keep going when I am not feeling my best. To me, it is all about making sure that when the chance to win a Stanley Cup ever comes again, I will be ready for it."

And if that ever happens again, you can be sure that Darcy Kuemper will make sure that the people of Saskatoon will get to share in his success. And you can also be sure that he will be eating more pierogies out of the Stanley Cup.

CHAPTER 19

Hague Family Matters

2023 Vegas Golden Knights
Nicolas "Nic" Hague

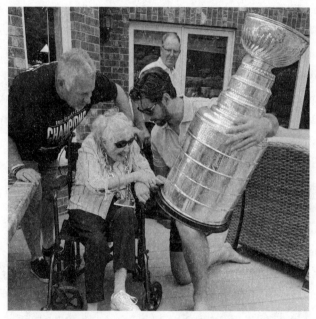

Nic Hague's grandma finds his name on the Cup while his dad watches

For Nic Hague of the 2023 Vegas Golden Knights, his dream turned into a reality that was far better than anything that he ever imagined.

"During the playoffs, I would be sitting on the couch, watching TV, and my mind would start to wander. I would be thinking about lifting the Stanley Cup over my head, and the team celebration afterwards. I was thinking of the parade and how great it would be."

What Hague never anticipated during all of his dreams was the stress that comes when closing out the biggest playoff series of one's career.

"In game five of the Stanley Cup Final, we had a three-to-one series lead. I scored the second goal of the game. At the start of the third period, we had a six–one lead. We knew we were going to win the game and win the series, but the final twenty minutes of game five felt like it took over three hours to play. The clock moved in slow motion that period and when the game finally ended, it was the greatest sense of relief that you could imagine."

To Hague, his dreams never truly came close to what it felt like to be a Stanley Cup champion.

"I couldn't comprehend how impressive it actually was when we won. The real thing was so much better than anything I ever imagined. I will admit, winning the Cup was very emotional to me. I must have cried at least eight times within twenty-four hours of us winning. We went out all night after we won and the next day I woke up and looked at my girlfriend, Ally, and said to her, 'Did we really just do that?' She looked at me said, 'Yes, you really won the Stanley Cup.' We were both hungover, so I wasn't sure."

Sunday, August 27, 2023, was a textbook-perfect summer morning in Kitchener, Ontario. Hundreds of fans decked out in Golden Knights gear lined the parking lot at the Activa Sportsplex, patiently waiting to meet Nic Hague and the Stanley Cup. All of this took place just a few weeks after he got engaged to his girlfriend.

"This summer had been nuts."

After signing countless autographs and taking photos with as many people as humanly possible, Hague, his family and friends, the Stanley Cup, and the Keeper of the Cup hopped on a party bus and headed to his parents' home.

Two of the Keepers of the Cup were on duty for Nic's day. The head Keeper, Phil Pritchard, was there, and one of his top assistants, veteran Walt Neubrand, was also there to watch over the proceedings. Another thing Nic's dream didn't prepare him for was the feeling of elation that washed over him as he celebrated his day with the Stanley Cup in his parents' crowded backyard.

"You look outside of my parents' backyard and see my family and friends, that's what this day mean to me. Being able to share the Stanley Cup with the people that I love most in the world, and enjoy the day, is an incredible feeling. I have had so much support over the years from my family. Even playing in Vegas, being so far away from home, not everyone gets to see me. After we won the Stanley Cup, my mom and dad and my girlfriend, Ally, were the only three people that got to share the Cup with me that night. So, for me to bring the Cup home to Kitchener, and share it with everyone else, that is what it is all about for me."

Taking the Stanley Cup to his parents' house had an intense impact on Nic Hague.

"When I had my day with the Stanley Cup, that is when it really sunk in that we did it. Sitting here in my parents' house with the Stanley Cup is so cool. I grew up in this house. We had the Cup in Vegas and had fun and all that. But I grew up here, so to have the Cup in the backyard of my parents' house, it is all kids' dream come true."

The star of the show was Nic's ninety-nine-year-old grandmother. Because she is in a wheelchair, Nic decided to invent a way for her to drink out of the Cup. His dad, Bob, grabbed a straw and they poured some white wine into the bowl and as Nic held the Stanley Cup, Grandma Hague took a long drink.

To Nic, having his family, and especially his grandmother, there with him, celebrating and drinking out of the Cup, was a priceless moment.

"My grandmother will turn one hundred years old later this year, and for her to be here today, and drink wine out of the Stanley Cup, it blows me away. I am going to go out on a limb and say she might be the oldest person ever to drink out of the Cup. My grandpa passed away in 2016, and to have his motorcycle parked in the driveway and being able to sit on it with the Stanley Cup means so much more to me than money or fame. This day is all about sharing the Stanley Cup with the people that are the most important to me, and that is my family."

One thing that was new in 2023 was that the NHL and the Hockey Hall of Fame had all the names of the Golden Knights players, coaches, management, and staff engraved on the Cup *before* the start of the summer tour. That meant players were able to show off their name on the Cup to family and friends.

"My grandmother made me laugh. She looked at me and said, 'Why is my name on the Stanley Cup?' I told her, 'It is because we share the same last name,' and her eyes lit up. From moments like that, to the scrapbook my mom made, chronicling our run to the Stanley Cup. That surprised me when I got back home to Kitchener. Things like that, and to have everyone we love sharing the day with us. Our family name, my name, will be on the Stanley Cup forever; that is pretty cool. It is a name that I share with everyone that I hold dearly in my life. The Stanley Cup is such a historical trophy, and it brings smiles out in everyone."

Nic said there was one thing that kept him and his Golden Knights going during the long grind of eighty-one regular-season games and another twenty-two playoff games.

"Winning a Stanley Cup is not an easy thing to do. You do get beat up mentally and physically along the way. You have to deal with ups and downs throughout the playoffs. You lose a game, you win a game, you have to move on and get ready for the next game and the next series. It is something that I never understood until I went through it. Our team found a way to manage all of those ups and downs this year, and we were able to win it all. But the grind that we go through to win a Stanley Cup, it makes that day that you get to share with your family and friends all the more fun."

Nic's mom, Sheila, was busy preparing his all-time favorite snack food to eat out of the Cup.

"I am going to eat buffalo chicken dip out of the Stanley Cup. It is not a secret recipe by any means. I am quite certain the recipe is on the back of the Frank's RedHot bottle. It is something that my mom always made when I was growing up, and it always has been one of my favorite snacks."

One of the hardest things, Nic Hague admitted, was trying to pick a picture that best summed up what winning the Stanley Cup meant to him.

"A couple days after we won the Stanley Cup, we were going through some photos. I felt like I said at least five hundred times, 'Oh, we should frame that one!' The second time that I had a turn with the Stanley Cup after we won, I was with my parents. I handed the Cup to my dad. He looked confused and I told him, 'Dad, lift it up!' He picked it up over his head and someone took a photo of the two of us at that moment.

"The night we won the Stanley Cup was very emotional," he continues. "To be there with my mom and dad, and my girlfriend at the time and now my fiancée, it was a ton of fun. These are the people that I lean on the most in life. And I was lucky enough to share that moment with them."

Nic Hague might still be a young player, but he is wise enough to understand the impact the Stanley Cup has on everyone who gets near it.

"That Cup, I have to tell you, it just brings out something special in people. It is a lot of fun to be around and witness other people's joy spending time with it."

The kind of fun and joy that you can't even dream about.

CHAPTER 20

He's Got Your Back

Rocket
Watcher of the Players and the Cup

Rocket with Sidney Crosby (*left*) and Nathan MacKinnon

Rocket isn't his real name. But to his friends and to his clients, that is what he's known as. Like a lot of Canadian kids, Rocket grew up playing hockey. He even played AAA hockey with Paul Coffey as a member of the Mississauga Reps tyke team.

Years later, as an adult, Rocket had a friend who owned a company in Toronto that oversaw security for all of the concerts that came into the city. Out of nowhere, Rocket received an offer he couldn't refuse.

"I was in the music industry, and I used to work for all of these bands," says Rocket. "I used to work for a local guy in Toronto, Ross Renzetti. Ross had a company that managed security for bands and musicians, and he asked me to do some security for him. Along the way, I got to know Gil Gamboa. Gil was with Bruce Springsteen at the time. Gil asked me to come out on the road with Bruce and handle security for him during his tour. The biggest thing that helped me get to where I am today is the fact that I have a clean record. A lot of security personnel that worked in the United States had drug charges or drunk driving charges. Because of that, they couldn't get into Canada to work. Whenever a band or a musician was about to tour Canada and their head of security was unable to travel to Canada, they would call me. I ended up getting so much work because of that.

"If I have one skill, I am good with people," Rocket continues. "A band would come into Toronto, and I would deal with their security guy. I would help them get whatever the band needed, and I knew the city. They would ask me, 'Where is a good place to eat for my band?' I would get asked about a lot of things and I would help them out. One day I was working security with Tim McGraw, and he said, 'Why don't you come on the road with me? I need someone like you.'"

That was the start of Rocket's journey into personal security for some of the biggest names in music. After Tim McGraw he worked with A-list stars like Bruce Springsteen, the Tragically Hip, Red Hot Chili Peppers, and Madonna. Wherever they went, you would find Rocket standing in the wings, watching over them like a sheepdog protecting his flock.

"I would do a lot of the local shows at the different venues in Toronto and a lot of hockey players would come to watch some music. When

I knew NHL players were at one of my concerts, I would take care of them while they were there and make sure that nobody bothered them." They were just music fans, trying to watch a show and have a fun time.

During a slow time, Rocket was asked to do security for NHL players. When young star players in the NHL wanted to go out to a concert in Toronto, Rocket would drive them to the venue, make sure there was no trouble, and then make sure they got home. "Over time, I got to know a lot of players in the NHL. Anytime someone needed something in Toronto, they would reach out to me. What I didn't realize is that my name was being circulated around the NHL. The word was out that if you were in Toronto and wanted to see a concert, you should get ahold of me. I bet ninety-nine percent of my NHL clients are all from word of mouth and referrals."

Currently, Rocket provides security for well over seventy players throughout the NHL.

Beginning in 2018, with select members of the Washington Capitals, Rocket started providing personal security for his clients' days with the Stanley Cup. He has been given a front-row seat to some amazing experiences.

"What happened was these Stanley Cup parties have started to get bigger and bigger," says Rocket. "The NHL suggested that it would be good to have extra security on hand at all times, to protect the player and the Cup. Every time a team wins the Cup, I get the call to help with security. I have done over two dozen parties and the numbers keep growing.

"Having me at these Stanley Cup events is good for the player, it is good for the Hockey Hall of Fame, and it is good for the league," relates Rocket. "The NHL asks for a security person to be present on the day. Not only do I know the players, but I also know good fans from bad fans, and I know when it is okay for certain fans to go over and say hi to the player and touch the Stanley Cup with them. I love working with all the of Keepers of the Cup. With me being there, it takes pressure off them, and I find that knowing they are there, I feel less pressure on the day. The rule is that no fan can lift the Stanley Cup over their head by themselves. I say this to every player that I have ever worked for, 'I will be the bad guy,' I am the guy that tells someone that they can't do that. At the end of the day, that is what I am paid for. When a player asks me to work security for them on their day with the Cup, I am there from seven in the morning when the Keeper of the Cup arrives, and I am still there at midnight when they pack up the Cup and take it away."

Rocket feels it only makes sense to have someone watching out for the player when they have their day with the Cup.

"The problem is the player has to look after his family, his friends, and even old coaches. I am the guy that will pull the player away from everyone and make sure they take a break."

The Stanley Cup is heavy, and it feels even heavier when a player has to lift it hundreds of times in a single day. "By the end of the day, a player's arms are exhausted, and their hands hurt. When the Cup is taken away there is a feeling of sadness, but also a chance to breathe after an exhausting day.

"I find the family and the friends of the players I am working with on their day with the Stanley Cup treat me so well," Rocket shares. "In fact, they are unbelievably kind and generous. They know that I am there to watch over their son. One mom told me once, 'As long as you are with him, I know my son is in good hands.' Most players pay me yearly, and that covers my expenses anytime that they need me to work security for them. Other players pay only when they need me. The biggest reason I am there is I am the guy that gets them out of there when they have had enough. I tell people, 'We have to go,' when I know the player needs to leave. Parents will come up to me and ask me, 'Rocket, my son needs to see his aunt, or his old neighbor,' and I take them away, so they have time to see everyone on their big day.

"This is something that I have learned over the years," says Rocket. "Rock stars want to be athletes or a hockey player, and hockey players and athletes want to be rock stars! However, security for rock stars and security for a hockey player is different. The hockey players are fan-friendly and generally they are good guys. Working with big rock stars trained me not to be starstruck when I am working with a client. When I work with a hockey player, I am not there to be in pictures. That is the player's day, not my day. I am happy to be in the background."

One of Rocket's favorite Cup Day experiences took place in the summer of 2022 as Nathan MacKinnon of the Avs gave Halifax and Nova Scotia a day to remember. "Nate and his family treated me with so much respect, you would think that I had won the Cup too. They couldn't do enough for me. Sidney Crosby was a part of MacKinnon's party, and he was first-class all the way. Sidney Crosby respects the Stanley Cup so much; it rubs off on everyone else."

No matter who it is, every player, past and present, has so much respect for the Stanley Cup.

"It is so hard to win the Cup. What they put their bodies through to win a Cup is insane. The average fan never sees that."

"Erik Johnson almost quit hockey, but he stayed and won a Cup with the Avs in 2022. For someone who waited so long to win, he was going to make sure to squeeze every second from his day with the Cup. One of the stops when Erik had his day with the Cup was Del Mar horse-race track in California. What a gong show! When we arrived at the track, Steve Kerr, the head coach of the Golden State Warriors, was there with the Larry O'Brien Trophy. We were in this little party room with over a hundred people in a room built to hold twenty! Erik was sweating so hard, he had to change his shirt three times. At the end of his day with the Cup, EJ [Erik Johnson] was so emotional. I was with Erik and Mike Bolt, and we walked back to put the Stanley Cup back in the road case. Erik hugged and kissed the Cup and had tears in his eyes. He went through so much in his career before he finally won a Stanley Cup. At the end Erik said, 'I will see you next year.' Then the Cup was gone."

Over the past few years, that has become a new tradition when a player says goodbye to the Stanley Cup at the end of their day. Before the road case closes, they look at the Cup and say, "I will see you next year."

Over the years, Rocket has developed a bond with his NHL clients beyond vendor and client. He sees things that nobody else will ever see and they trust him. Rocket also knows to never touch the Cup. "All of my clients who have never won the Cup yet, they wouldn't even shake my hand if they knew that I had touched it."

Players past and present are extremely superstitious about touching the Stanley Cup. "At Nathan MacKinnon's Stanley Cup party, we were in his backyard. All these people were drinking from the Cup and Nate's arms were beginning to get really sore from holding it all day. Nate was cradling the Cup as someone drank from it and it began to slip out of his arms. Nate threw the Cup towards Sid [Sidney Crosby] to catch it. Sid jumped out of the way, and it grazed his shirt. Sid hadn't won the Cup that year and he wouldn't touch it!"

Rocket knows how demanding a day with the Stanley Cup can be.

"For the player, that day with the Stanley Cup can be grueling. It is physically tiring because they are carrying the Cup around all day long. There are endless amounts of people who are trying to talk to the player and have their photo taken with them and the Cup. Everyone wants a piece of their time that day. It turns into a giant petting zoo with the player. By the end of the night, most people who are at the party have had too much to drink. It is a physically and emotionally tiring day. Eventually, the player needs a break from everyone so they can have fifteen minutes away from everybody. The drunker everyone gets, that is when people start to try and do stupid things with the Cup. And I am the only sober person there, and I am trying to protect the player and protect the Cup."

No matter what player he is providing security for, there is one person who seems to stand out above everyone else, and that is the player's mother.

"We were with Nathan MacKinnon and his sweet mom asked if we could drive by a local nursing home so this person could wave at Nate and the Cup as we slowly drove by. That was one of the nicest moments I have ever experienced."

During Rocket's time with the Cup, he discovered an intense un-written rule that is held near and dear to NHL players.

"Brad Marchand of the Bruins attended Nate's [MacKinnon] Cup party. Because Marchand had won a Cup before, he was allowed to be there, same thing as Sidney Crosby. Only a player who has won it is allowed to attend another player's Stanley Cup party."

Rocket has just about seen it all in providing security at Stanley Cup parties. He has been to a country music festival with Pat Maroon. He also watched NFL legend Peyton Manning attend the Avalanche Cup party in Denver. But the moment that meant the most to him was the time he spent with Nazem Kadri in summer 2022.

"Taking the Stanley Cup to the mosque in London, Ontario, with Nazem was neat. It had never been to a mosque before.

"Every player that I worked with will whisper in my ear, 'Hey, we are going to get the Cup a little longer, right?' And I will always tell them that when midnight comes along, you will be relieved to see the Stanley Cup get packed up and leave. At the end of a player's day with the Stanley Cup, they are physically and mentally exhausted. Every few hours, I pull the player away from what they are doing and make them take a break for about ten minutes.

"I love all of the Keepers of the Cup," says Rocket. "They are all such good people. There are times when the Keeper of the Cup and I will look at each other and say to each other, 'Can you believe how lucky we are?'

"When a player hires me to work security on their day with the Cup, I receive a game plan from the organizers. Every player who gets a day with the Stanley Cup has to have an organizer. It is like having a wedding planner. The Hockey Hall of Fame wants to have a fairly detailed itinerary of your day with the Cup, where it is going to be, and how long they expect to be at each event. The NHL and the Hockey Hall of Fame want to know where you are planning on bringing the Cup. The best part of the day always ends up being the quiet hour they spend with family and friends at their childhood home. I have been in Sidney Crosby's backyard in Nova Scotia. It doesn't get much better than that."

Wherever the Cup ends up in the future, you are likely to see Rocket standing in the wings, watching over the Cup, watching his respective client, and making sure there are no problems. "It is a very emotional day for everyone involved. It is emotional, and yet the day goes by extremely fast."

For Rocket, working security, protecting his players, and protecting his clients is a twelve-month-a-year job. While his clients party and have

Rocket with Phil Kessel

fun and drink champagne and beer out of the Stanley Cup, he carefully surveys his surroundings, making sure nothing happens to anyone. If it sounds like a demanding job, that's because it is. But it is also rewarding, and watching his clients enjoy the best day of their life, hanging out with the Stanley Cup, is the ultimate perk.

At the end of a long day, around midnight, when the Cup starts its journey to the next celebration, Rocket will see his clients watch the Stanley Cup being placed in the road case, and he'll hear them say the same thing: "See you next year."

Acknowledgments

I have so many people to thank in writing this book.

First off, I would like to thank my amazing wife and our two daughters for their never-ending support. Special thanks to our cat and dog, who never allowed me to stop working.

Thanks again to my consigliere, my trusted agent, Brian Wood. Thank you to Kevin Hanson, all the editors, and the entire team at Simon & Schuster Canada. It takes a great team to win a Stanley Cup and it took a great team to put together this book. I also thank the management and staff at my radio station, 105.9 FM The Region.

I would like to thank the following people who played a key role in helping me find all the current and retired players that are in the book: Andrew Jackson of Jackson Events; hockey historian and author Liam Maguire; Kevin Shea; Scott Harris; Matt Nichol; Bob McKenzie; and Karen Stock. Special thanks to Kelly Masse, Phil Pritchard, and everyone at the Hockey Hall of Fame. Thanks to Wade Arnott and the staff at Newport Sports. Thanks to the Nashville Predators, the Minnesota Wild, the Tampa Bay Lightning, the Pittsburgh Penguins, the Vegas Golden Knights, and the Toronto Maple Leafs. I also would like to thank Ben Hankinson at Octagon Hockey.

A big thanks to the following invaluable research websites: Hockeydb.com, NHL.com, Hockeyreference.com, TSN.ca, Sportsnet.ca, ESPN.com, and HHOF.com. Hockey fans are blessed to have so many great podcasts and I also found them to be an important resource. Shout-out to the *Cam and Strick* podcast, *Spittin' Chiclets*, *32 Thoughts*, *Speak of the Devils*, *Ray and Dregs*, *The Full 60 with Craig Custance*, and *ESPN on Ice*.

Most of all, I will be eternally grateful to all the coaches and players for taking the time to speak with me about one of the most important days in their lives, their day with the Stanley Cup. In no particular order, thank you to Scott Young, Mike Ricci, Mike Modano, Guy Carbonneau, Craig Ludwig, Fredrik Modin, André Roy, Bill Ranford, Brendan Shanahan, Sidney Crosby, Devante Smith-Pelly, Mike Vernon, Anders Eriksson, Mathieu Dandenault, Brad "May Day" May, Robert Thomas, Dan Hinote, Eric Messier, Johnny Boychuk, Rich Peverley, Jordan Nolan, Ken Daneyko, Randy McKay, Bill Guerin, Larry Robinson, Darcy Kuemper, Jon Cooper, and Nicolas "Nic" Hague. With big assistance from his parents, Bob and Sheila, and Grandma Hague. I would also like to thank Mike Bolt, Phil Pritchard, and Walt Neubrand from the Hockey Hall of Fame, the vaunted Keepers of the Cup. And last, but certainly not least, Rocket. A personal security expert, Rocket is the man most often watching over players when they spend their day with the Stanley Cup.

Photo Credits

I am indebted to the following for providing permission to reproduce the following photographs: Patricia Roelofsen (p. xvii); Mike Bolt (pp. 1, 3, 9); X (p. 11); Ken Daneyko (p. 15); Randy McKay (p. 23); Scott Young (p. 43); Mike Ricci (p. 44); Mike Vernon (p. 52); Anders Eriksson (p. 56); Mathieu Dandenault (p. 61); Mike Modano (p. 76); Guy Carbonneau (p. 72); Craig Ludwig (pp. 76, 79); Larry Robinson (p. 90); Dan Hinote (p. 98); Eric Messier (p. 105); Brendan Shanahan (p. 111); Fredrik Modin (p. 111); André Roy (p. 126); Brad May (p. 135); Pittsburgh Penguins (pp. 147, 150); Johnny Boychuk (p. 158); Rich Peverley (p. 163); Jordan Nolan and the Nolan family (p. 169); Bill Ranford (p. 177); Devante Smith-Pelly (p. 183); Robert Thomas/ Author (p. 191); Michael O'Halloran/Gabe Marte/Vinik Sports Group/ Tampa Bay Lightning (pp. 199, 203); Darcy Kuemper (pp. 211, 216); Nic Hague/Author (p. 219); and Rocket (pp. 225, 232).

Index

Note: Page numbers in *italics* indicate figures.